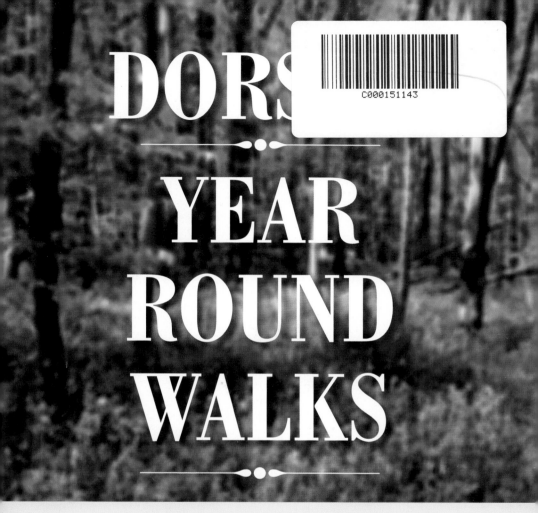

DORS[ET]

YEAR
ROUND
WALKS

Spring, Summer, Autumn & Winter

Anne-Marie Edwards

COUNTRYSIDE BOOKS
NEWBURY BERKSHIRE

First published 2018
Text © 2018 Anne-Marie Edwards

COUNTRYSIDE BOOKS
3 Catherine Road
Newbury
Berkshire

To view our complete range of books please visit us at
www.countrysidebooks.co.uk

ISBN 978 1 84674 352 8

Photographs by Mike Edwards and Julie Edwards

Produced by The Letterworks Ltd., Reading
Typeset by KT Designs, St Helens
Printed by The Holywell Press, Oxford

Contents

Contents

Autumn

Winter

Introduction

Dorset, with its glorious coastline and gentle rolling hills, is a walker's county. In its many quiet villages and small market towns, often tucked away in wooded valleys, life still moves at the pace of the walker, rather than at that of the car. The countryside is infinitely varied and often spectacular; it is said that after a tour of Dorset, you will have seen three quarters of England!

In this collection of walks, I take you to some of my favourite places. These include hilltop villages on Cranborne Chase; historic settlements in the Tarrant Valley; Eggardon, famous for its wonderful views; the magnificent Purbeck coast; and the Vale of Blackmore, with its high-hedged lanes and flower-filled meadows.

All of the walks follow historic rights of way which have been established by people in the course of their everyday lives, as they walked to work, to church, to market, to the nearest inn or to visit friends. The walks can be enjoyed throughout the year, but for this book I have grouped them by the seasons to which I feel they are most appropriate. In spring, Hod Hill is golden with cowslips, Abbot Street Copse near Pamphill is a sea of bluebells, and cygnets play in the streams at Abbotsbury Swannery. On a fine day in summer, there are wonderful views west over the Jurassic Coast from Swyre Head in the Purbeck Hills, and the heathland near Bere Regis is purple with heather. Autumn brings colour to Beaminster woods, and Stanpit Marsh Nature Reserve near Christchurch is a splendid place to see migrant birds. And to appreciate the special atmosphere of Eggardon Hill, you must walk the ramparts in winter.

The walks are all circular, and range from two to six miles in length. They are accompanied by simple sketch maps designed to guide you to the starting point and give an overall picture of the route. For more detailed information on a particular route, I recommend you arm yourself with the relevant Ordnance Survey map, which is noted in the introduction to each walk.

Dorset countryside can become muddy even after light rainfall, so it is best to wear boots or strong shoes when walking. In our fickle climate, it is usually wise to carry a waterproof with a hood and to wear long trousers, not shorts. (Dorset nettles favour the sides of footpaths!) On even a short walk, I always take a drink and a sustaining snack. I wish you many happy hours exploring this enchanting county.

Anne-Marie Edwards

Acknowledgements
As always, I am most grateful to the rest of the team: my husband Mike and our daughter Julie, who walked with me and took the photographs. Without them this book would never have been written.

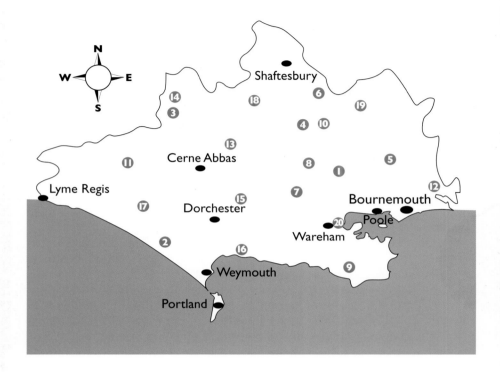

PUBLISHER'S NOTE

We hope that you obtain considerable enjoyment from this book; great care has been taken in its preparation. Although at the time of publication all routes followed public rights of way or permitted paths, diversion orders can be made and permissions withdrawn.

We cannot, of course, be held responsible for such diversion orders and any inaccuracies in the text which result from these or any other changes to the routes, nor any damage which might result from walkers trespassing on private property. We are anxious though that all the details covering the walks are kept up to date and would therefore welcome information from readers which would be relevant to future editions.

The simple sketch maps that accompany the walks in this book are based on notes made by the author whilst surveying the routes on the ground. They are designed to show you how to reach the start and to point out the main features of the overall circuit, and they contain a progression of numbers that relate to the paragraphs of the text.

However, for the benefit of a proper map, we do recommend that you purchase the relevant Ordnance Survey sheet covering your walk. Ordnance Survey maps are widely available, especially through booksellers and local newsagents.

Little Pamphill

1 Pamphill

4.5 miles / 7.2 km

There is nowhere quite like Pamphill, where you start this superb walk. As part of the vast Kingston Lacy Estate, now bequeathed to the National Trust but owned for many years by the Bankes family, the village has slumbered peacefully through the centuries almost untouched by time. Here there is no recognisable village street, only a scattering of mainly deep-thatched, half-timbered cottages and farms set among the open greens of a still medieval landscape. From the village the walk descends into the Stour Valley to follow the riverside rich in wildlife before crossing an ancient green and taking a sunken path back to Pamphill. But before you reach the village a path leads you to the highlight of this walk, Abbot Street Copse.

DORSET *Year Round Walks*

Terrain Easy walking, apart from one gentle uphill.

Map OS Explorer 118 Shaftesbury & Cranborne Chase.

Starting point Pamphill Green car park (GR ST 991008).

How to get there Pamphill is about a mile west of Wimborne Minster. From Wimborne Minster, take the B3082 in the direction of Blandford. Just after the Pamphill Dairy sign, turn left for Pamphill, Cowgrove and Kingston Lacy church. Pass Pamphill Dairy on the right and a lane to Pamphill Farm on the left, and take the next left in front of the church. Pamphill Green car park is on your right. **Sat Nav:** BH21 4ED.

Refreshments The Parlour Café at Pamphill Dairy serves morning coffee, lunch and teas ☎ 01202 857131. The Vine Inn serves traditional ales and meals ☎ 01202 882259.

The Walk

❶ From **Pamphill Green car park** turn right to walk over the grass of the cricket field with the road close by on your left. You will see the small thatched cricket pavilion ahead. Join the road and continue past **Pamphill school car park** on your left. Now **Pamphill First School**, the building you see on your left has an interesting history. Endowed by Roger Gillingham, it was built in 1698 with a school in the higher classical centre flanked by eight single-room almshouses. When you have passed the school the road divides.

❷ Take the left-hand road signed for the **Stour Valley Way**. Just past a parking area for the **Vine Inn** on the right, turn right up the lane to **Little Pamphill**, a delectable group of colour-washed cottages standing high on a ridge with beautiful views over the **Stour Valley**. Bear left to complete a circle and return to the road opposite the **Vine Inn**. We were surprised to see the cottages in this tiny place were numbered in the five hundreds! Evidently the Bankes family numbered all the houses on their estate consecutively and as their lands extended south to the Purbecks you will find number one in Studland. Turn right to leave the **Vine Inn** on your left and continue downhill to a road.

❸ Cross the road and go through the squeeze stile opposite. Bear right over the field towards a farm gate passing a cottage on your right. Go through another squeeze stile beside the gate and keep ahead under a height restriction barrier to the parking area at **Eyebridge**. Walk down to the river, the site of an ancient

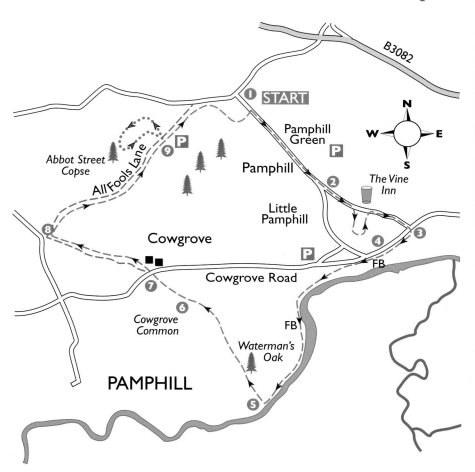

ford, now crossed by a modern footbridge. An information panel describes life here in Roman and medieval times.

4 Do not cross the bridge but turn right to follow a beautiful path following the riverside. The river is on your left. The **Stour** runs slowly between grass-covered banks and overhanging bushes and trees which provide food and shelter for a wide variety of wildlife. You will find tempting seats at intervals along the riverside. Pass a path on your right and cross a bridge to continue beside the river.

5 The path bears right here away from the river to run through woodland

Bluebells in Abbot Street Copse

and you have a choice of routes. You can follow the upper narrow path beside a fence or a parallel lower track on your left which can be muddy. The paths wind north past some magnificent trees, among them a splendid oak known as **Waterman's Oak** reputed to be over three hundred years old. Keep straight on past a squeeze stile and footpath on your right and when the upper path becomes overgrown continue along the lower track.

6 Leave the woods to follow a path which bears right over a small bridge to bring you to the edge of **Cowgrove Common**. Follow the path ahead over the common with a tiny stream on your right and go past a gate to **Cowgrove Road**. A thatched, half-timbered house is on your right and opposite is **Poplar Farm**.

7 Cross the road to the track in front of **Poplar Farm**. **Cowgrove Pond** is on your left. Turn left along the gravel track marked with a blue arrow bridleway sign to leave the farm on your right and the pond on your left. Keep straight ahead passing a squeeze stile and footpath sign on your right. The track runs past a cottage on the right and continues over an open green, past a house on the right.

8 Immediately past the house you meet a road. Do not follow the road but turn right up **All Fools Lane** (a footpath) signed for **Pamphill**. This path dates from Saxon times and was originally All Souls Lane as it once led to a chapel at the top of the hill. Follow the path uphill until you see a small iron gate on your left.

9 Turn left through the gate and cross the field to go through a second gate into **Abbot Street Copse**. The copse is famous for its sea of bluebells in spring and has an interesting history. The trees conceal the embankments of the first 'Kingston', a royal residence built by the Saxon king Ine in the seventh century. Follow the path straight ahead across the copse before it curves left to bring you back to the iron gate. Retrace your steps over the field to return to **All Fools Lane** and turn left. Just before you meet the road turn right over the grass then right again to return to **Pamphill Green car park**.

spring

What to look out for –

River wildlife

The Stour is exceptionally rich in wildlife. The number of otters is increasing and if you do this walk at a quiet time there is a good chance you may see one. Listen for its loud chirping cries. You may also see water voles. Kingfishers perch on overhanging branches above the water and herons stand watching in the shallows. The banks are colourful with wild flowers including marsh marigolds, purple loosestrife and water forget-me-nots. Among the butterflies they attract are the peacock and orange tip. Shortly after the end of the surfaced path look for the large wooden carving of an otter holding his fish on the left of the path. Apart from his size he is very lifelike!

The Fleet at Abbotsbury.

2 *Abbotsbury*

3 miles / 4.8 km

There is so much to enjoy as you follow the route of this walk that you need a whole day to ensure you don't miss anything! The route starts in Abbotsbury, a beautiful and historic village set comfortably in a sheltered hollow of the coastal downs at the western end of the Fleet, an eight-mile-long tidal lagoon. The houses and cottages are built of golden stone and many date from the 16th and 17th centuries with wooden casement windows and reed-thatched roofs. Benedictine monks founded an abbey here in the 11th century and among the remains of the abbey are the massive tithe barn and the chapel of St Catherine on the top of Chapel Hill. The monks established a swannery on the reedy shores of the Fleet, an ideal situation protected from south-westerly gales by the Chesil Bank. After 600 years, the swannery still flourishes under the protection of the Strangways family. These can all be visited on this rewarding walk.

Terrain Easy walking, apart from one short climb.

Map OS Explorer OL15 Purbeck & South Dorset.

Starting point Abbotsbury village car park (GR SY 578852).

How to get there Abbotsbury lies on the B3157 coastal road between Weymouth and Bridport. Turn off the B3157 for the car park, following the sign 'For village and children's farm'. **Sat Nav:** DT3 4JL.

Refreshments There are various cafés and tea rooms in Abbotsbury village. The swannery also has a café ☎ 01305 871190.

The Walk

1 From the car park return to the road, the B3157.

2 Turn left to walk through the village. The road is now called **Rodden Row** and is lined with shops and cottages. All are different and all have their own character. Some have heavy buttresses and stone-mullioned windows and some have carved stones in their walls taken from the remains of the abbey after the Dissolution in 1539.

3 At the T-junction ignore the signs indicating left for the swannery and turn right up **Market Street** past the 18th-century **Ilchester Arms** on your left. Follow the road round to the left past **Strangways Hall**.

4 Opposite **Red Lane**, just before the **Post Office**, look carefully for a finger post on the left indicating, among other signs, your destination, **Chapel Hill**. Turn left along the track with a hedge and low wall on your right. The village is left behind and you are instantly in the countryside. Occasionally through the trees you catch glimpses of **St Catherine's Chapel** on the top of **Chapel Hill**.

5 As you reach the foot of **Chapel Hill** there are three possible paths. Take the middle path and keep ahead, following the sign on the finger post for **St Catherine's Chapel**. Go through a squeaky gate and climb the hillside up a clear path to the chapel. You need to walk carefully as the hillsides are terraced with strip lynchets, dug in medieval times when arable land was scarce.

6 The Chapel is well worth the climb! It was built by the monks in the late 14th century as a seamark and chantry for sailors, entirely of stone. Even the roof

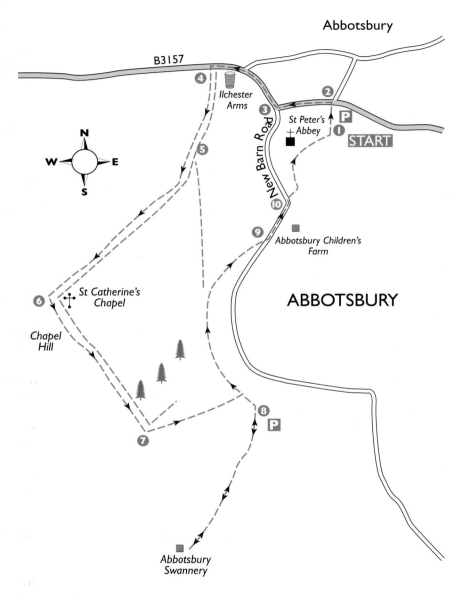

Abbotsbury

B3157

Ilchester Arms

St Peter's Abbey

START

New Barn Road

N
W E
S

Abbotsbury Children's Farm

ABBOTSBURY

St Catherine's Chapel

Chapel Hill

Abbotsbury Swannery

is stone and the walls are four feet thick! It was too useful to be destroyed and so survived the Dissolution. The views from this exposed hilltop are spectacular in all directions – inland over Abbotsbury cupped in the downs, over the Fleet to Portland and west over Lyme Bay. Walk round to the seaward side of the

spring

14

Looking south-west from Chapel Hill.

chapel. The route now runs down the south-east side of **Chapel Hill**. There is no clear path at this point but go through a gate in the fence surrounding the chapel and you will see a finger post on the corner of the fence on your left. Follow the direction downhill for the swannery. Pick your way carefully round the lynchets! About halfway down the hill look down to a wood and continue aiming for the right-hand edge. Just before you reach the wood there is a seat. Look ahead for two large stones a little to your left indicating your way to the swannery. Go down the hill to the first stone and turn left to follow the arrows to the swannery past the second stone.

7 Keep ahead over two stiles to the corner of **Grove Lane** near the swannery buildings.

8 In the shop you can buy your tickets to visit the swannery, the only colony of nesting mute swans where you can follow pathways among the birds. In May and June hundreds of cygnets play around the paths and in the pools and creeks. The swannery is well signed and there is an informative leaflet with a map. After your visit retrace your steps to **Grove Lane** and keep ahead to meet **New Barn Road** near the tithe barn.

DORSET Year Round Walks

9 Turn left along **New Barn Road**. The former abbey's tithe barn is on your right overlooking one of the abbey's fish ponds. It is a huge building only part of which is thatched. Inside there is a fascinating museum housing agricultural implements used by our ancestors and a children's farm where under-eights can cuddle guinea pigs, race toy tractors and bottle-feed the baby lambs.

10 When the road kinks left, turn right following a green sign indicating the footpath to the village car park, to walk along the northern side of the pond. Turn left uphill to the church. The church dedicated to St Nicholas dates from the 16th century and, among many interesting features, it possesses a panelled Jacobean pulpit with a high back. In the pulpit's canopy are two bullet holes made by Cromwell's men during the Civil War when the church and nearby manor were held for the King with disastrous consequences for the defenders. Leave the church by the south porch and follow the path back to the village car park where this walk began.

What to look out for –

Abbotsbury Swannery

The whole family will enjoy a visit to the swannery. Children can help to feed the swans at mass feeding times, and listen to a microphone commentary by the swanherd. Among many attractions there is a giant swan maze where children have to find their way to a giant egg at the centre, pedal go-karts and a delightful swinging nests play area near the café. Frankie the barn owl gives a fascinating flying display from May to September. Every half-hour you can watch an audiovisual show *A Year at the Swannery*.

The swannery is open every day from March to October from 10am to 5pm. The Swannery Café is open from 10am to 4.30pm. The site is fully accessible for disabled visitors. You can buy a Passport Ticket which allows you to visit the swannery, children's farm and  the nearby subtropical gardens at a reduced rate.
www.abbotsbury-tourism.co.uk/swannery

The magnificent west front of the 15th-century tower of the church of St Mary, Bradford Abbas.

3 Bradford Abbas

4 miles / 6.4 km

Although this lovely walk in the Blackmore Vale can be enjoyed throughout the year the lush countryside of the Vale is at its most beautiful in late spring. Bradford Abbas, where the route starts, is one of Dorset's most attractive villages built of golden stone from Ham Hill. In the 15th century the wool trade brought prosperity and the village is famous for its magnificent church of St Mary which dates from that time. The west front of the tower is decorated with 11 canopied niches, two of which contain their original figures. Inside there is much to admire including a 15th-century stone rood screen.

From the village the route follows meadow paths and lanes bordered with wild flowers to Thornford a small village built along the crest of a hill with a glorious view far over the valley of the river Yeo to the Somerset hills. The route follows the river for part of the way to return to Bradford Abbas.

17

DORSET *Year Round Walks*

spring

The Facts

Terrain One short climb; otherwise flat, easy walking.

Map OS Explorer 129 Yeovil & Sherborne.

Starting point Parking in Church Road near Bradford Abbas church (GR ST 587142).

How to get there Bradford Abbas is three miles south-east of Yeovil. Approaching from the south along the A37, take the turning for Yetminster, then head north to cross the River Yeo. Take the next turning on the left, which is signed for Bradford Abbas Village Hall and leads to the church. Alternatively, approaching from the north via the A30 Yeovil–Sherborne road, take the turning south, signposted for Bradford Abbas. Then turn right, following the sign for Bradford Abbas Village Hall. The road leads to the church. **Sat Nav:** DT9 6RF.

Refreshments The Rose and Crown in Bradford Abbas serves food all week. The Village Store serves coffee and afternoon teas. The Crown in Thornford serves lunch and dinner.

The Walk

1 With the south face of the church on your left, walk down the village street past the **Rose and Crown** and the **War Memorial**. Opposite the village store you will see a narrow path running between stone walls on your right.

2 Turn right to step over a low iron stile and follow the path which leads through a small gate to meadows bordering the **River Yeo**. Keep ahead (left-hand path) with a stone wall at first on your left. Go through a gate and cross over a road. Go through a gate and keep straight on along a track.

3 Navigate carefully at this point! Just before you come to the mill buildings turn right to leave the track and then turn left to walk along the crest of a grassy slope leading down to the river with a hedge on your left. The path bears a little right over a footbridge then curves left between posts. Follow the path as it continues over another footbridge and through a gate to a field. A clear path leads ahead. Although we could see no sign, the remains of a six-room Roman villa were discovered nearby. A gate leads into a meadow.

4 At first the path ahead is not clear. But, if you look over the meadow a little to your right, you will see two farm gates in the hedge. Beyond them, on the top

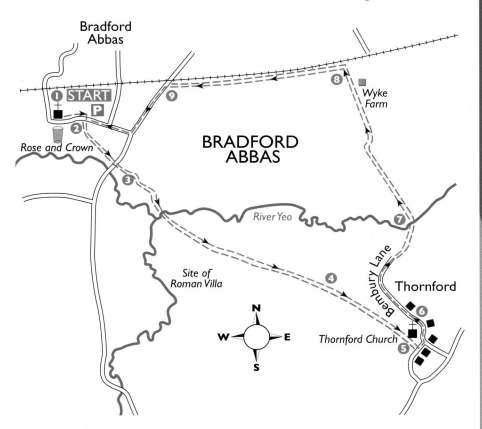

of a rise, is the tower of **Thornford church**. Make your way over the meadow towards the farm gates and go through the small gate beside them. Follow the path across the next field and go through the gate. Walk up the rise ahead to **Thornford church**. Look back to enjoy the splendid view.

5 Go through a gate and, leaving the church on your left, walk beside the churchyard wall to a road in **Thornford** village. Bear left and follow the road as it curves right.

6 Turn left down **Bembury Lane**. This pleasant lane curves right past **Bembury Farm** and becomes a grassy track leading ahead through the trees beside the Yeo. Just before you come to a footbridge over the river you will find an ideal spot for a picnic – a seat on the riverbank overlooking the river, which runs sparkling over a low waterfall alive with dragonflies.

7 Turn left to cross the footbridge and two smaller bridges and go through a gate to a field. Follow the narrow path as it leads ahead beside fields with a hedge on the right. After crossing a small bridge, the path continues between hedges to a gate on your right. Go through the gate and bear left up the field with a hedge about 40 yards away on your left and a fence on your right. Cross a stile by a gate and follow the path past a large thatched barn. A little further on, as you approach the railway crossing gate, you will catch a glimpse of medieval **Wyke Farm** beyond its walls on your right.

8 Just before the railway crossing gate turn left through a small gate to walk along the edge of fields through gates to a road. The railway is on your right.

9 Turn left down the road then turn right following the sign for **Bradford Abbas Village Hall**. Follow the road to return to the church and your car.

What to look out for –

Thornford

The centre of Thornford near the church has been declared a conservation area and is well worth exploring. The church dedicated to St. Mary Magdalen dates back to Norman times and has a 14th-century chancel and tower. Look in the chancel for a small window showing a sparrow pulling a harrow in memory of Dr Sparrow who was a vicar of Sherborne in the 15th century. The table tomb near the south porch has a small hollow on the top. Evidently tenants could place five shillings in the hollow to stop the Lord of the Manor from taking tithes of hay – part of their harvest owed by law to the Lord of the Manor – during the year. The money had to be in place before 12 noon on St. Thomas' Day (21 December). Records show that the Lord of the Manor and the vicar, (who supported the tenants) once took the matter to court. The vicar lost. The imposing brick clock tower was erected to commemorate Queen Victoria's Diamond Jubilee in 1897. Later inscriptions commemorate the Silver Jubilee of King George V in 1935 and the installation of lighting in Thornford by public subscription as a tribute to those who died in the Second World War.

Cowslips on Hod Hill.

4 Stourpaine and Hod Hill

4.5 miles / 7.2 km

Hod Hill is one of Dorset's treasures. Set high above a meander of the Stour, it is crowned with the ramparts of the county's largest Iron Age hillforts. From Stourpaine, an attractive village set in a wooded valley, this magnificent walk leads up the hill to cross the fort, still dotted with the hollow circles and ridges of Iron Age houses, then follows the encircling ramparts offering splendid views. In the north-west corner the path leads past the rectangular embankments of a large Roman fort built by the second legion Augusta after they captured Hod Hill in AD43. You can enjoy this walk throughout the year but Hod Hill is a wonderful place to be in spring, when a carpet of golden cowslips is followed by orchids and a host of other downland flowers attracting many rare butterflies including the Adonis blue.

DORSET *Year Round Walks*

Terrain One gradual climb up Hod Hill; an undulating path along the ramparts.

Map OS Explorers 117 Cerne Abbas & Bere Regis, and 118 Shaftesbury & Cranborne Chase.

Starting point Stourpaine church (GR ST 861094).

How to get there Approaching from the south, follow the A354 for Blandford Forum, then continue along the A350 in the direction of Shaftesbury. Pass the turning on the left for Sturminster Newton and keep going, following the signs for Stourpaine. In the village, turn left after the White Horse pub, then left again to the church, where there is room to park. **Sat Nav:** DT11 8JZ.

Refreshments The White Horse is a traditional, welcoming village pub dating from the early 18th century; it has an inglenook fireplace and two dining rooms. ☎ 01258 453535.

The Walk

1 Leaving the church on your right, walk down the road ahead. This is a very attractive part of **Stourpaine** with many thatched cottages and flower-filled gardens. At the crossroads, keep straight on along **Manor Road**. The brick wall of the manor is on your right. Opposite the manor entrance you can visit a little garden. It is a peaceful place with clipped box hedges enclosing beds of lavender and a waterfall playing into a pool. Return to **Manor Road** to continue the walk, leaving the garden on your left.

2 When the road swings right, keep straight on along a gravelled track which curves left to bring you to a sign pointing right for **Hod Hill**. Turn right as directed to follow the footpath beside the Iwerne stream which, at first, is on your left. The stream runs under a bridge to continue on your right.

3 The path widens to meet another footpath leading ahead. Do not follow this but leave the streamside and bear left up the track which climbs the side of **Hod Hill**. As you climb you are rewarded with beautiful views over Stourpaine and the Stour Valley. The track brings you to a gate and stile in front of the outer ramparts of the **Iron Age fort**.

4 Cross the stile and follow the path which weaves through the ramparts

spring

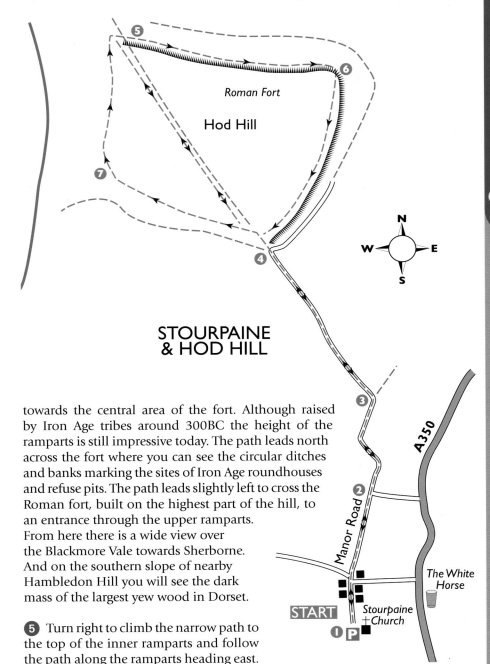

Roman Fort

Hod Hill

STOURPAINE
& HOD HILL

N
W — E
S

A350

Manor Road

towards the central area of the fort. Although raised by Iron Age tribes around 300BC the height of the ramparts is still impressive today. The path leads north across the fort where you can see the circular ditches and banks marking the sites of Iron Age roundhouses and refuse pits. The path leads slightly left to cross the Roman fort, built on the highest part of the hill, to an entrance through the upper ramparts. From here there is a wide view over the Blackmore Vale towards Sherborne. And on the southern slope of nearby Hambledon Hill you will see the dark mass of the largest yew wood in Dorset.

The White Horse

START   Stourpaine
         ✝Church

5 Turn right to climb the narrow path to the top of the inner ramparts and follow the path along the ramparts heading east.

There are gaps at times in the ramparts and you will need to walk down then up again to rejoin the path.

6 Keep to the ramparts as they curve south to run down to Point 4 (where you entered the fort). Cross the path and continue heading west along the southern ramparts. The south-west corner of the hillfort has been excavated and it is believed that the Iron Age chieftain's hut stood here, destroyed by Roman ballista bolts. Unlike Maiden Castle there are no signs of a battle on Hod Hill. Perhaps the defenders were taken by surprise and quietly left before the Roman onslaught.

7 Follow the ramparts as they curve north to Point 5 where you began the **Hod Hill circuit**. Turn right to retrace your steps following the path across the fort to go through the gate and turn right by the **Iwerne** to return to **Stourpaine**. Find time if possible to visit the church of **Holy Trinity** which has many interesting features, including a fine pulpit, designed and carved by local people.

What to look out for –

Hod Hill Roman Fort

The Roman fort built in the north-west corner of the Iron Age fort on Hod Hill is fascinating. Originally a wooden stockade would have surmounted the rectangular earth embankments. The three entrance gates were each equipped with a watchtower and a platform for artillery. Excavations of the fort have revealed that, inside the defences, rows of timber barrack blocks housed around 500 foot soldiers and larger buildings a cavalry unit of about 300 men. The headquarters and hospital stood either side of

a main road. The fort also had a granary, storehouse, commander's house, toilets and a large water tank. As the route of this walk crosses the fort it is possible to make out the shape of some of the buildings. Excavations also suggest that the fort was used as a base for about seven years until around AD50 when troops were withdrawn for the campaigns against Caractacus in the west and the remaining men were moved to a new fort at Waddon Hill above the present-day village of Stoke Abbott.

In Ferndown Forest.

5 *Ferndown Forest and Uddens Water*

4.5 miles / 7.2 km

All the family will enjoy this ramble crossing the woods and heathland surrounding the valley of Uddens Water. Although within easy reach of Bournemouth and Poole the countryside is surprisingly remote and rich in wildlife. The walk starts in White Sheet car park north of Ferndown. White Sheet Plantation is owned by the Forestry Commission and is a beautiful area of attractive mixed woodland and open heath. Wet areas are noted for dragonflies and a wealth of birdlife including hobby, hen harrier and merlin. After taking a path heading south through the trees of the plantation, the route continues heading south across the Uddens Water valley, once an estate owned by the now-demolished Uddens House. Park Copse and Garden Copse beside the route have retained their original names. Leading south-east the route crosses a footbridge over Uddens Water to join the Castleman Trailway, one of east Dorset's most delightful long-distance footpaths and cycleways. After following the trail through the trees of Uddens Plantation the return route crosses the open heathland of White Sheet Plantation to return to the car park. This is a walk you can enjoy throughout the year, but it is particularly rewarding in spring when the cuckoo calls through the woods and the heath is starred with wild flowers.

spring

The Facts

Terrain Easy flat walking.

Map OS Explorers OL22 New Forest, and 118 Shaftesbury & Cranborne Chase.

Starting point White Sheet car park, White Sheet Plantation (GR SU 048037).

How to get there Follow the A31 to the Ringwood roundabout, and take the exit for Ashley Heath, Three Legged Cross and Horton. Continue along the Horton road through Three Legged Cross, and turn left shortly after the village, following the sign for Holt. The road now runs for a little while beside Holt Heath. Then turn left, following the sign to Broom Hill, Colehill and Wimborne Minster. (The signpost is on the right, just past the turning.) After about ¾ mile, turn left into White Sheet car park. **Sat Nav:** BH21 7DB.

Refreshments The family-friendly Three Legged Cross inn is around 4 miles away in Wimborne. ☎ 01202 826052.

The Walk

1 Walk back towards the entrance to the car park. Before you get there you will see a grassy footpath leading south through the trees on the left. Turn left and follow this path passing a Forestry Commission barrier on your left. Through a fringe of trees on your right you will glimpse farmland at first but shortly the path leads more deeply into the woods with a fence on the left. Follow the line of the fence past another Forestry Commission barrier and a gate on the left.

2 The path bears left beside the fence then curves right in front of a gate following the line of the fence to bring you to a wide gravel track running along the southern edge of the fenced plantation. Turn left and follow the gravel track for about a quarter of a mile to the first track on your right.

3 Turn right to follow this way through the former parkland surrounding **Uddens House** leading between the trees of **Park Copse** and **Stable Copse**. The track continues past the more open area of **Garden Copse** and crosses **Red Bridge** over a small tributary of **Uddens Water** to bring you to a lane.

4 Continue along the lane to a Public Footpath sign on the right pointing left indicating a path across the grassy verge.

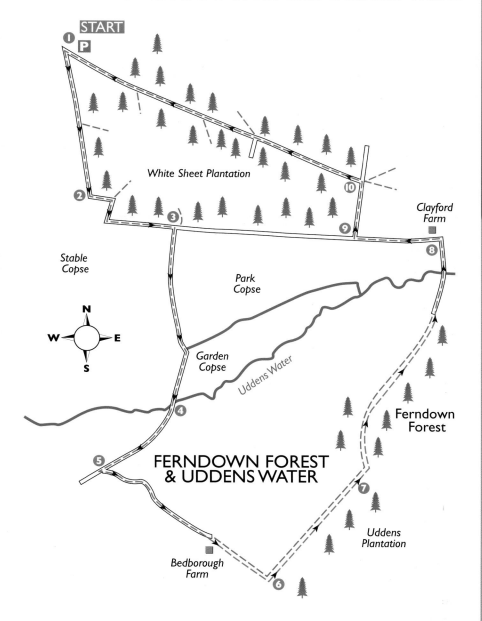

START
P

White Sheet Plantation

2

3

10

Clayford
Farm

9

8

Stable
Copse

Park
Copse

N
W   E
S

Garden
Copse

Uddens Water

4

Ferndown
Forest

5

**FERNDOWN FOREST
& UDDENS WATER**

7

Uddens
Plantation

Bedborough
Farm

6

5 Navigate carefully at this point! Turn left across the verge as indicated along a very faint path leading towards woodland. Pick your way into the woods and a clear path leads ahead through the trees. You are now following part of

Crossing Uddens Water.

the **Ferndown, Stour and Forest Trail**. The trail is a circular 10-mile footpath starting in **Ferndown** and weaving through forest and across heath to follow the banks of the **River Stour** before returning to **Ferndown** across farmland. Follow the trail as it winds through the trees to bring you to open farmland. Keep straight ahead to pass the buildings of **Bedborough Solar Farm** and go through a gate. Continue ahead through another gate leading into **Uddens Plantation**.

6 Turn left past a post on the left marked with the blue sign for the **Uddens Water Cycle Circular** to follow the route of the **Castleman Trailway**. (The **Ferndown, Stour and Forest Trail** follows the **Trailway** at this point.) The route leads ahead through the attractive mixed woodland of **Uddens Plantation**.

7 Cross the footbridge over **Uddens Water**. Our route leaves the **Castleman Trailway** which bears right to follow **Uddens Water**. Turn left, still following the **Ferndown, Stour and Forest Trail** through the trees of **Uddens Plantation**. Leave the woods to pass a Forestry Commission barrier and continue ahead to a crossing track in front of **Clayford Farm** buildings.

8 Leave the trail, which curves right and turn left to follow the track along the southern edge of **White Sheet Plantation**. Continue past all the buildings and houses on your right to a blue bridleway sign and gate on your right.

9 Go through the gate to follow the bridleway over the heath. Navigate carefully at this point! Continue over a grassy path (if you look right you will see it finish) and turn left along the first wide gravel track.

10 Keep ahead along the gravel track over all crossing tracks. After a final crosstrack our way leads a little uphill towards a gate. Go through the gate and after a few yards turn right through the trees to **White Sheet car park**.

What to look out for –

Castleman Trailway

The Castleman Trailway is 16 ½ miles long, running from Upton Country Park near Poole to the River Avon near Ringwood. Much of the way the Trailway follows the route of the former Southampton to Dorchester railway completed in the mid-19th century. The line was closed by Dr Beeching in 1964 but the Trailway, as it keeps to its route, provides a splendid opportunity for walkers, cyclists and horseriders to enjoy some of East Dorset's finest scenery.

The Trailway is named after Charles Castleman, a Wimborne solicitor, who was chiefly responsible for building the line. Locally the line is known as Castleman's Corkscrew after its founder and the meandering route it was forced to take to avoid valuable woodland, considered at that time to be far more important! Look for the Castleman Trailway's distinctive sign, a steam engine on a footprint.

Approaching Ashmore Wood.

6 Ashmore

4.5 miles / 7.2 km

Ashmore is one of the most fascinating of Dorset's many secret villages. A rare survival of a Celtic hilltop settlement, it is the highest village in the county commanding wonderful views of the western downs of Cranborne Chase. The houses, many of which are thatched, cluster around a large dew pond which is home for a noisy tribe of mallard and Muscovy ducks. Their playground seldom dries as the early hilltop settlers lined their pond with clay. From the village the route crosses the downs to Ashmore Wood. In summer the wood is full of wild flowers and you can still find some magnificent trees, reminders of the great forests that once covered the Chase. After leaving Ashmore Wood, our path follows the edge of Mudoak Wood to cross the route of a Roman road. More woodland ways lead back to the village.

Terrain Easy walking, with one short climb.

Map OS Explorer 118 Shaftesbury & Cranborne Chase.

Starting point Parking beside Ashmore pond (GR ST 912178).

How to get there Ashmore is a small village in north-east Dorset, about four miles south-east of Shaftesbury. Approaching from Shaftesbury, head south on the A350 and turn left in Fontmell Magna for Ashmore. The best approach from the south is to take the A350 north from Blandford Forum, turning right in Fontmell Magna for Ashmore. **Sat Nav:** SP5 5AD.

Refreshments Good, home-cooked food is served all day at the Fontmell pub in Fontmell Magna, about four miles from Ashmore ☎ 01747 811441.

The Walk

① With the pond on your left, and the houses of the village on your right, follow the road past the **War Memorial**. Continue past the church gates. As the road curves right, turn left along the bridleway signed for **Ashmore Wood**. (**Halfpenny Lane**.) Follow the bridleway as it runs high over the down towards **Ashmore Wood**. The path runs into the wood to a crosspath.

② Turn left along the bridleway signed for **Well Bottom**. (**Elderen Row**.) Among the trees on the left look for some splendid beeches. In early summer the trees shelter a sea of bluebells, to be followed by white anemones and tall stands of foxgloves. Follow the woodland path as it descends into the valley at **Well Bottom**.

③ Bear a little left up a lane passing **Spring Farm** on the left. Follow the lane uphill.

④ Just past the drive to **Well Bottom Cottage**, turn right along a lane signed for **Mudoak Farm**.

⑤ Navigate carefully at this point! Our way is a grassy footpath on the left just before you come to a track to a large barn. Turn left to follow the path with tall pine trees on the right and open fields on the left. The pines give way to a tall hedge and the path curves a little right to go through a gate. Follow the path

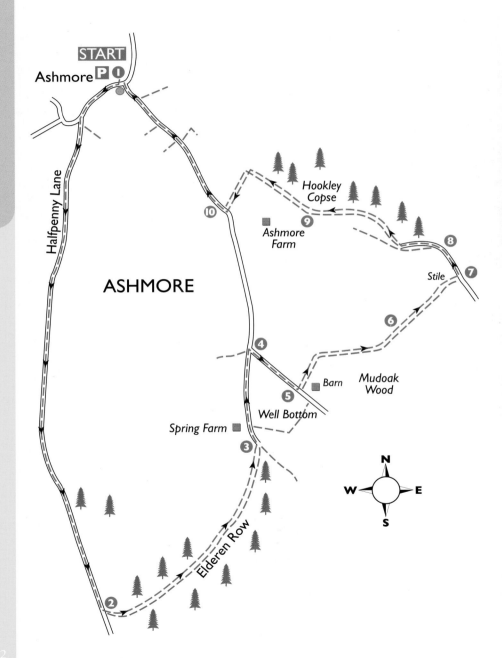

START

Ashmore 🅿 ❶

summer

Halfpenny Lane

ASHMORE

❿

Hookley
Copse

■ Ashmore
Farm

❾

❽

Stile

❼

❻

❹

■ Barn

Mudoak
Wood

❺

Well Bottom

Spring Farm ■

❸

Elderen Row

❷

N

W ─ E

S

Ashmore pond.

along the fringe of **Mudoak Wood** with a row of tall beeches on your right. This is a lovely walk – much better than the name of the wood would suggest!

6 As you approach the eastern edge of **Mudoak Wood** look for an arrow on the left directing our way into the wood. At this point, turn left into the wood for a few steps then bear right to leave the trees and emerge on a good track. There is a gate for **Ashmore Farm** on the left. Bear right through a similar gate and take the good track leading downhill between a hedge on the left and fields on the right. (As you leave **Mudoak Wood** you cross the line of the Roman road which ran from Hamworthy on Poole Harbour via Badbury Rings to Bath.)

7 At the foot of the field cross a stile (the footpath signs are illegible) to join a bridleway. Turn left and keep ahead past a bridleway on the right to a junction of several paths.

(8) Keep ahead along the bridleway leading just within the left-hand edge of **Hookley Copse**. The bridleway winds round the edge of the copse, then continues between wattle fencing on the left and hedges on the right.

(9) (At this point the path differs a little from the OS map, which shows the diversion to avoid Ashmore Farm running through woodland.) Our path turns sharp right then almost immediately left between hedges on the left and open fields on the right. A final left turn brings you to a lane by **Ashmore Manor**.

(10) Turn right to follow the lane through the village to return to your car.

What to look out for –

Carvings and stones from the ruins of Eastbury House

When Eastbury House, a great mansion near Tarrant Gunville, was demolished many of the stones and carvings found their way into the villages on Cranborne Chase. As you walk through Ashmore look out for unusual decorative features. On the right-hand gable end of Manor House Farm you will see a delicate band of corbelling which probably came from Eastbury House. If you go through the church gates and walk towards the church you will see a beautiful round carving in the wall of a house on the right.

'Filly Loo'

In 1956 an ancient custom was revived at Ashmore called the 'Filly Loo', which probably means 'uproar'! The festival is held on the Friday evening nearest to the feast of St John the Baptist or Midsummer's Day. The villagers form a procession and dance to music provided by a local band and the day ends with a torchlit procession led by six 'deer-men', complete with antlers, and characters from Dorset folklore including an archer, a rider on a hobby horse and a fool.

The Bere Stream is a nature reserve

7 *Bere Regis*

5 miles / 8 km

Great areas of wild heathland once stretched across Dorset immortalised by Thomas Hardy as 'Egdon'. Much has become pine forest but south of Bere Regis, between the Bere stream and the Puddle river, you can still walk on the beautiful open heathland that Hardy knew. The heath is at its best when purple with heather making this ramble in Hardy's footsteps a perfect walk for late summer. The route starts close to the church in Bere Regis and follows the Bere stream to Shitterton, a lovely corner of old Dorset with thatched, colour-washed houses. From the village, you follow the Jubilee Trail along sunken paths leading up the heath giving glorious views, before descending into the Puddle Valley close to Turners Puddle, a tiny hamlet by the riverside. The route leaves the Jubilee Trail to cross the heath by different paths and return to Bere Regis.

The Dorset Jubilee Trail is 90 miles long. It was established to celebrate the 60th anniversary of the founding of the Ramblers Association and opened in 1995.

Terrain Some gradual climbing, but generally easy.

Map OS Explorer 117 Cerne Abbas & Bere Regis.

Starting point The car park near the church in Bere Regis (GR SY 847948).

How to get there Bere Regis is on the A35, roughly halfway between Dorchester and Poole. Approaching from the east, turn left for Bere Regis off the A35, just before the junction with the A31. Turn left again, following the road sign for Wool, passing the Royal Oak on your right. After about 50 yards, turn right into Elder Road. Another right turn shortly afterwards takes you to the car park on your right. **Sat Nav:** BH20 7HA.

Refreshments The Royal Oak in Bere Regis is a former coaching inn, dating from early in the 17th century ☎ 01929 471203.

The Walk

❶ From the car park follow the sign 'To the Church'. After passing some houses the path leads through a gate into the churchyard. Find time to visit this splendid church, one of the most beautiful in Dorset. After your visit, turn left from the south porch and walk down to the **Wool** road.

❷ Look across the road. In the field opposite King John held court – so Bere became Bere Regis! The grassed-over foundations you may see in the field are the remains of a manor house built by the Turberville family, who were lords of the manor of Bere Regis for 500 years from the 13th to the 18th century. Turn right down the road and after a few yards turn right again to follow **Elder Road** until you come to **Manor Farm Road** on the right.

❸ Turn left over the grass towards the **Bere stream**. Do not cross the bridge but bear right along the footpath beside the stream which is on your left. This clear chalk stream and its surroundings are a nature reserve. Among the birds you may see are kingfishers, herons and grey wagtails. The footpath leads to a boardwalk which carries you dry-shod over marshes colourful in season with water mint and yellow flag irises. As you come to drier ground the boardwalk gives way to a path. Continue heading west past a bridge on the left to a lane in **Shitterton**.

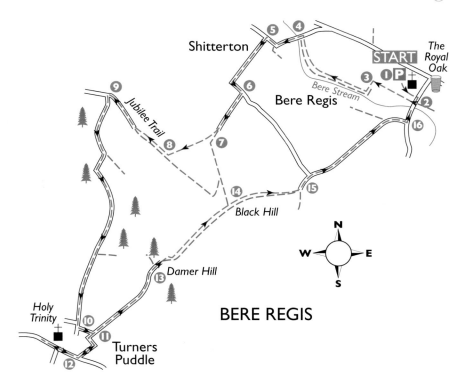

Shitterton

Bere Regis

Black Hill

Damer Hill

Holy
Trinity

BERE REGIS

Turners
Puddle

The
Royal
Oak

Bere Stream

N
W — E
S

④ Turn left along the lane to cross a bridge over the **Bere stream** and walk through the village. The lane curves right past a footpath on the left. Continue along the lane.

⑤ Opposite house **number 7**, turn left up the signed footpath to follow the Jubilee Trail. The sign for the trail is a small circular disc with a green arrow on a white background. Follow the sunken track, which becomes a narrow grassy path between hedges, as it leads gradually uphill to a crossing path. Turn left and keep ahead for about 150 yards to a junction.

⑥ Turn right uphill towards the heath beneath pollarded hazels to a small iron gate.

⑦ Go through the gate and turn right up a permissive path following the **Jubilee Trail** sign. After a few yards the path divides in front of hollows. Bear right and keep to the narrow path which dips and winds up the heath to meet a wide green crosstrack.

A barn in the Puddle valley.

⑧ Turn right to follow this ridge path to enjoy fine views north over the **Bere stream** and south over the **Puddle Valley**. Keep ahead through a gate until you come to a crosspath with a track leading ahead to a farm.

⑨ Turn immediately left to follow a pleasant path which curves right then left to bring you downhill into the **Puddle Valley**.

⑩ A few yards before you see a gate leading to farm buildings, turn left following a sign through a gate along a narrow footpath. This leads through a metal gate and over a farm track to go through a wooden gate to a signed green crosstrack. (We rejoin this crosstrack on our return route.)

⑪ Turn right and follow the path which curves left then right to go through a gate to a lane in **Turners Puddle**.

⑫ To see the tiny church turn right past the farm. The church stands on a grassy terrace overlooking the river. Some of the names on the gravestones – Talbut and Chamberlayne – are reminders of King John's visits to Bere Regis. Retrace your steps along the lane, to follow our outbound footpath to the signed green crosstrack at Point 11. Pass the wooden gate on your left and keep ahead along the green crosstrack which climbs gradually through woodland.

⑬ Keep ahead past a footpath on the left and shortly after, pass a footpath on the right. The path leaves the woods. A short steep climb brings you to the top of **Damer Hill**. Go over a crosstrack and follow the level path ahead over a crosspath to **Black Hill**.

⑭ Pick your way downhill round the humps and hollows of **Black Hill** to an iron gate that you will see on your left at the foot of the hill.

⑮ Bear left through the gate to take the downhill path ahead passing three paths on your left. The path descends past houses. Keep straight on down to a road and follow the road round to the right, past the drive to the primary school on the left, to the **Wool** road.

⑯ Turn left up the road to the lane on your left leading to the church. Retrace your steps across the churchyard to return to the car park.

What to look out for –

Bere Regis Parish Church

Thomas Hardy set some of the scenes in his novel *Tess of the d'Urbervilles* in this splendid church slightly altering the name of a real family, the Turbervilles. The family vault lies just to the right of the south porch. In the novel, the homeless Durbeyfield family set up their four-poster bed on the grass above overlooked by the Tudor window bearing the Turberville crest and coat of arms. Tess recalls that her family have a seal and a spoon with these insignia. Inside the church, there is a great deal of interest but its glory is the magnificent 15th-century roof of the nave. It is constructed entirely of oak with brightly painted figures of the twelve apostles dressed as Tudor gentlemen leaning at right angles from their supports  as if keeping an eye on the congregation. The roof was the gift of Cardinal John Morton, Archbishop of Canterbury and Chancellor to Henry VII. The Cardinal was born in the parish.

Crawford bridge over the Stour.

8 Spetisbury and Tarrant Crawford

4 miles / 6.4 km

Spetisbury is an attractive village built along a ridge overlooking meadows threaded by the river Stour. The nine arches of Crawford Bridge, dating from early in the 15th century, carry the road from the village over the Stour to the Tarrant Valley. This little chalk stream rises in the hills of Cranborne Chase and flows south for ten miles giving its name to eight villages before it meets the Stour near Spetisbury. From the village, this walk follows raised footbridges to an old mill then leads over the watermeadows to the Tarrant Valley. Here, in an idyllic setting beside the river, stands the 12th-century church of St Mary the Virgin decorated with medieval wall paintings. Even today it can only be reached by a bridleway! You return to Spetisbury over Crawford Bridge to take the trailway along the track of the former Somerset and Dorset railway past the station which is being restored.

Terrain Easy, almost flat walking.

Map OS Explorer 118 Shaftesbury & Cranborne Chase.

Starting point Clapcott's Farm (GR ST 910030).

How to get there Spetisbury is a linear village beside the A350, about four miles south-east of Blandford Forum. Clapcott's Farm is at the north end of the village. Approaching from the north, turn left down a lane signposted to the Old Mill. Clapcott's Farm is a few yards down the road, on the left. Park in the large parking area. **Sat Nav:** DT11 9DF.

Refreshments Clapcott's Farm has a shop selling locally-produced food, and serves breakfast, light lunches and teas with home-made cakes ☎ 07771 774006.
The Woodpecker pub serves lunch Tuesday–Sunday and dinner Tuesday–Saturday. The pub is closed on Monday ☎ 01258 452658.

The Walk

1 Pass **Clapcott's Farm** on your left and keep ahead along a narrow footpath on the left. This leads you over long footbridges crossing tributaries of the **Stour** and the mill pond to the **Old Mill**.

2 Turn left in front of the millhouse and look for a narrow paved path on your left leading ahead beside a brick wall. Turn left to follow this path which leads through woods then over a bridge to a gate opening to the Stour watermeadows. Go through the gate and keep ahead over the meadows crossing more bridges to go over the **Stour** to **Keynston Mill**.

3 Navigate carefully at this point as our way is unsigned. Leave the millhouse on your left and turn left up the gravel drive. After about 50 yards you will see a narrow tarmac path on the right. Leave the drive and follow this path for a few yards up to a raised bank. Turn right to walk along the top of the bank. You pass some wooden posts on the left. The path continues beside fields with a thick belt of woodland on the right. Keep to the path as it curves left and right to bring you to a large iron gate in front of a road. Beside the gate a signpost indicates the way you have followed as a bridleway (open for walkers, horse riders and cyclists only). Another bridleway sign points over the road to a drive.

4 Cross the road and follow the drive. The 'Private Road' notice only applies

summer

to motorised vehicles as it is a bridleway. (Cars may follow it to visit Tarrant Crawford Church.) The drive runs between fields on the left and trees concealing the Tarrant on the right. Also hidden from sight at this point are the remains of a great Cistercian abbey for nuns founded in the 13th century by Richard Poore, Bishop of Durham and Salisbury, who was born locally. Pass a drive to **Abbey House** on the right following the sign 'To the Church'. The drive curves right to cross a bridge over the **Tarrant** to a track by the churchyard gate.

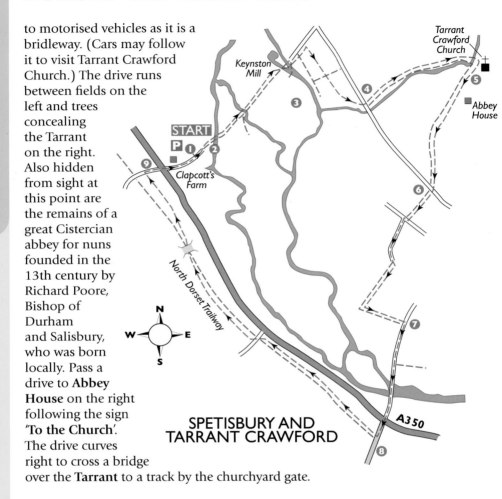

SPETISBURY AND
TARRANT CRAWFORD

5 The tiny church of **St Mary the Virgin**, surrounded by fields and woodland, is another of Dorset's treasures. It has been aptly described by Frederick Treves in *Highways and Byways in Dorset* as 'a village church of olden days'. Leave the church to retrace your steps through the churchyard gate. With your back to the gate follow the track ahead for about 50 yards to an iron gate on your left. A broad track between fences runs diagonally up the hillside. (You will see the small blue arrows marking a bridleway.) Go through the gate and follow the track up the hillside. In the valley you can see some of the former abbey's ruined buildings including the great barn. Go through a gate and follow the field path ahead through more gates to a minor road.

6　Cross the road, go through the gate and follow the field path down the field into the **Stour Valley**. Follow the bridleway signs to walk down the next field. Cross a lane and keep ahead with a fence on the left. The bridleway curves left then right down a field then bears left to bring you to a road.

7　Turn right and follow the road over **Crawford Bridge** to the A350 which runs north-west through **Spetisbury**. Cross the road and walk up the road ahead. After a few yards look for the trailway sign on your right.

8　Turn right and follow a narrow tarmac path winding uphill to bring you to the track of the former **Somerset and Dorset railway**, now a trailway running between high embankments parallel with the A350. Turn right along the track. Occasionally through the trees on the right you will glimpse the rooftops of the village. Spetisbury Station is being restored by volunteers and after about half a mile you will see the up and down platforms and part of the station with its sign. There is a delightful picnic area with a small wooden train, the Pines Express, complete with its bell. An information board gives details of the restoration work so far. Continue along the track for about another half mile. Go under a railway bridge and shortly after you come to a signpost on the right pointing down a footpath on the left indicating 'Footpath 10'. Look ahead along the track and you will see some wooden fencing which marks the point we leave the **Trailway**.

9　Bear right by the fencing and follow the path down to the road. Turn right past the school car park, cross the A350 and follow the lane ahead to **Clapcott's Farm** and your car.

What to look out for –

Tarrant Crawford Church

The walls of this small church are almost entirely covered by medieval wall paintings, some may date from as early as the 13th century. A long sequence of paintings depicts the life of St Margaret. The south wall has two sets of paintings one above the other. The lower set shows three kings meeting three skeletons. This is believed to be a warning to the rich! Queen Joan of Scotland, daughter of King John and the wife of Alexander II, is buried here. She was the first abbess of the nearby abbey.

Looking west from Swyre Head over Kimmeridge Bay and Lulworth Cove.

9 Kingston and Swyre Head

3 miles / 4.8 km

This is a walk you must not miss. Swyre Head is the highest point on the seaward-facing Purbeck Hills and the views of Dorset's magnificent Jurassic coastline from the summit are breathtaking. And there is more to enjoy as you follow the route of this short walk. Nearby Kingston is an unspoilt Purbeck village, built and roofed with the local dove-grey limestone, standing high on a ridge overlooking Corfe Castle. The route crosses the open downland of the Encombe Estate to give you a perfect view of one of Dorset's loveliest valleys known as the Golden Bowl. Encombe House with its orchards and gardens, lies at the heart of the valley beside the wooded banks of a stream. The house was built by John Pitt whose father bought the estate in the mid-18th century. A gentle climb brings you to Swyre Head. The return route follows a ridge path with more spectacular coastal views before taking a quiet farm track back to the car park. This is a perfect walk for a summer evening.

The Facts

Terrain Easy walking.

Map OS Explorer OL15 Purbeck & South Dorset.

Starting point Swyre Head car park near Kingston (GR SY 943792).

How to get there Drive through Corfe village heading south on the A351. Turn right for Kingston along the B3069. At the end of the road, turn right past the Scott Arms pub along West Street, and continue along the road for about a mile, past Houns-tout car park, until you reach Swyre Head car park on the left. **Sat Nav:** BH20 5LP.

Refreshments The Scott Arms in Kingston has a garden with a splendid view of the ruins of Corfe Castle ☎ 01929 480270. There are other excellent pubs in Corfe village.

The Walk

1 Turn immediately left from **Swyre Head Car Park** between two stone gateposts, the entrance to one of the approaches to **Encombe House**. Cross the drive and grass, bearing a little right, to an iron gate by a signpost marked '**Bridleway to Swyre Head**'. Go through the gate and follow the clear stony path leading gently up the grassy slope ahead. The path curves right and leads through a gate at the top. Follow the path along the crest of the down with a stone wall and the trees of **Polar Wood** on your right. A beautiful view of the **Golden Bowl valley** sheltering **Encombe House**, framed by the sea, opens on your left.

2 After a few yards you will see a stone seat set back from the path on your right. It has been placed there, overlooking the sheer hillsides of the **Golden Bowl**, by the Royal British Legion. The seat is inscribed 'In Memory of those who gave their lives in flying accidents at this spot'. These included a Swordfish from the Torpedo Training unit in Gosport and the passengers and crew of a Liberator from Transport Command.

3 The path curves slightly left as it leads uphill to the grassed-over mound of a large tumulus at the top of **Swyre Head**. Climb the tumulus to enjoy the wonderful views. Looking west over **Kimmeridge Bay** and **Lulworth Cove** with **Portland** a dark shape on the horizon you can see as far as **Dartmoor**. To the east **St Aldhelm's Head**, with its ancient chapel and row of coastguards' cottages, dominates the coastline. Inland you have a wide-ranging view across

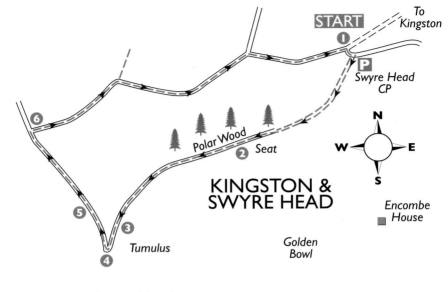

Swyre Head

the **Purbeck Hills** and **Nine Barrow Down** to **Poole Harbour**.

④ With your back to the tumulus walk straight ahead passing the trig point on your left. Pass a stile leading to a permissive path on your left and keep ahead to a gate marked as a public bridleway. Go through the gate and follow the field path along the crest of **Smedmore Hill** with more lovely coastal views. A low stone wall is on your left.

⑤ Continue along the hilltop following the field path and go through a second gate, appropriately named '**Heaven's Gate**'. I suggest you take a break here and enjoy the view looking west from a conveniently placed seat on the left. Smooth hillsides, dotted with woodland, slope down to the sea. Among the trees you can see **Smedmore House**, a large country residence built by Sir William Clavell in the early 17th century. The house is now privately owned. On the clifftop you will see Clavell Tower, strangely reminiscent of a pepperpot. It was built as a folly by Reverend John Richards Clavell. It has been renovated and moved a little further inland by the Landmark Trust and is now let as a holiday home.

⑥ Turn right past the marker stone for **Kingston** and go through the gate. Follow the grassy path ahead which slopes down to a farm track. The track

Tumulus at the top of Swyre Head.

curves right to go through a gate. Keep to the track as it bears a little left to a lane. Turn right and follow the lane to return to the start of the walk, **Swyre Head Car Park** and your car.

What to look out for –

Encombe House

This fine house, decorated with porticoes and columns, has a romantic story to tell. In 1807, the Encombe Estate was bought by the Lord Chancellor, John Scott, who took the title Earl of Eldon. John Scott's life reads like a fairytale. A poor boy, born in Love Lane in Newcastle, he fell in love with a rich banker's daughter, Bessie Surtees. The parents of both objected to their marriage so, with the aid of a ladder and an old friend, he eloped with Bessie and married her in Scotland. He made a fortune as a lawyer and remained devoted to his Bessie all his life. After a time, Mr Surtees was reconciled with his daughter.

Our inviting path to New Barn.

10 Tarrant Gunville

4 miles / 6.4 km

The rolling uplands of Cranborne Chase are wonderful walking country with widespread views over the downs and valleys sheltering many attractive villages. This walk, in the north of the Chase, starts at Tarrant Gunville, close to the source of the Tarrant stream. All the houses and cottages are different! Some are banded brick and flint, others have cob walls and many are thatched. Once the village had a forge, a shop, a post office, a school and a pub, the Bugle Horn. These may have gone but the houses retain their names. From the village, the route follows grassy tracks high on the downs giving splendid views. Buzzards soar overhead and in summer the grass is colourful with wild flowers. You return to the village through the parkland surrounding the remains of a once great mansion, Eastbury House.

The Facts

Terrain Easy walking.

Map OS Explorer 118 Shaftesbury & Cranborne Chase.

Starting point Roadside parking close to Tarrant Gunville village hall (GR ST 925129).

How to get there Tarrant Gunville is best approached via the A354, the Salisbury–Blandford Forum road. Approaching from Salisbury, turn right at the sign for Tarrant Hinton, and continue up the valley for about 1½ miles to Tarrant Gunville. Just past the phone box on the left, turn right and park by the road, near the village hall. **Sat Nav:** DT11 8JN.

Refreshments Home Farm is nearby, signed from the village. The tea room is open all year for breakfast, lunch and tea. The farm shop is stocked with locally produced foods. For opening times ☎ 01258 830083 or go to www.homefarmshop.co.uk.

The Walk

1 From the roadside parking walk to the main road. Turn right to walk through the village. Except in the height of summer, the little **Tarrant** stream runs under bridges on your left. Continue up the road as far as **Marlborough Farmhouse** on the right.

2 Beside **Marlborough Farmhouse**, turn right up the lane. (No sign, but it is a right of way.) Past the buildings, the lane becomes a track. Go through a gate and follow the grassy way ahead which rises gradually up the down, bordered by high hedges wreathed in summer with wild clematis and honeysuckle. Keep ahead past a wood on the right to meet a made track.

3 Turn left and follow the track for about a quarter of a mile to a junction of four ways.

4 Navigate carefully here as the way is not immediately obvious. Turn right through a gate to follow the grassy path ahead with trees on the left and a hedge on the right. You are now high on the downs with fine views. Continue past a wood on the left to a junction of several ways in front of a large barn on the right. (**New Barn** on the OS map.)

5 Turn sharp right, keeping the entrance and side of the barn close on the

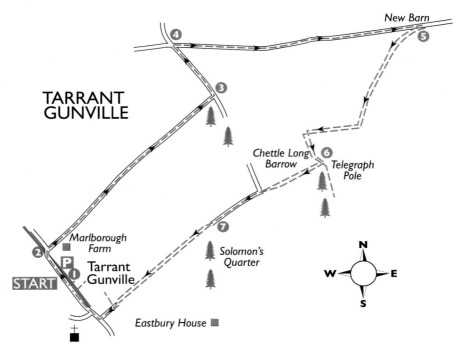

New Barn

TARRANT
GUNVILLE

Chettle Long
Barrow

Telegraph
Pole

Marlborough
Farm

Tarrant
Gunville

START

Solomon's
Quarter

Eastbury House

N
W   E
S

right, to go through a gate. Follow the path ahead beside a field with a hedge on the left. At the end of the field you reach a crossing hedge. Turn right to follow the path with the hedge on your right and a field on your left. The path turns left round the foot of the field, with the hedge still on the right, towards **Chettle Long Barrow**. The mound of the long barrow is heavily overgrown but it is still visible. At the approach to the barrow you will see a prominent telegraph pole marked with a blue arrow bridleway sign and a yellow arrow footpath sign.

⑥ Turn right following the yellow arrow footpath sign through a gap in the hedge to go through a small iron gate. The path bears left for a few yards, curves right round the foot of a field then follows the field edge with a hedge on the right. A splendid view over the **Tarrant valley** opens ahead. As you descend you come to a narrow asphalt track. At this point the track lies on the route of a Roman road that ran south from the Wiltshire border down the Tarrant Valley on its way to Badbury Rings and Poole Harbour. Cross the track and keep ahead along a grassy path between hedges. On the left, an area known as **Solomon's Quarter** reveals two symmetrical lines of round burial mounds dating from the Iron Age.

⑦ The path turns left through a small iron gate then immediately right

Meadow scabious beside our path.

and becomes a narrow path leading between a fence on the left and a hedge on the right along the edge of **Eastbury House parkland**. On the left a magnificent avenue of trees runs parallel with the path. If you look across the park, beyond the avenue of trees, you will catch a glimpse of the entrance to this once great house. Follow the path round to the left to go through a gate and bear right through a wood to a lane. Follow the lane to the **Tarrant Valley road** and turn right. Across the road you will see a white-walled cottage, which was formerly the village forge. On the wall is an old AA road sign recalling the early years of motoring. Follow the road to return to the village hall and your car.

What to look out for –

Eastbury House

Very little remains of this once magnificent mansion designed by Vanbrugh to rival Blenheim Palace. The house was built in the early 18th century for George Bubb Doddington and took 20 years to complete. After his death, and that of his nephew, the house passed to Earl Temple who had no need of a second residence. It was so large and expensive to maintain that no-one wanted to buy it and most of the building was demolished. Today only the stable block, which has been converted into a house, and the impressive gateways remain. Some of the great house's decorative features found their way into neighbouring villages! www.nationaltrust.org.uk/eastbury-manor-house

The AA sign

Before the last war the Automobile Association had erected nearly 30,000 signs in villages and towns. With the threat of invasion, most were removed and today there are probably only about 65 still in their original place around the country.

The view towards Gerrard's Hill.

11 Beaminster

2.5 miles / 4 km

Beaminster, where we begin this walk, is a small market town tucked in a green hollow in the West Dorset hills. Little seems to have changed in this delightful town with its friendly old-fashioned shops since the days of Thomas Hardy. The houses and cottages are built of creamy orange limestone and mostly date from Georgian times. They reflect the prosperity the town once enjoyed producing woollen cloth and goods made from locally grown hemp and flax. From the town, the route follows a streamside footpath then runs uphill, giving wide views over the Brit Valley and surrounding hills. The way continues through and old oak and beech wood, a quite magical place, especially when colourful in autumn. A path along the Brit Valley leads back to the town.

autumn

The Facts

Terrain One short climb; otherwise flat, easy walking.

Map OS Explorer 116 Lyme Regis & Bridport.

Starting point Yarn Barton car park, Beaminster (GR ST 481014).

How to get there Beaminster is on the A3066 between Bridport and Crewkerne. Approaching from the west, take the B3163 from Broadwindsor. To approach from the east, turn off the A356 to head for Beaminster along the B3163. Drive into the square and follow the sign for the Yarn Barton car park. **Sat Nav:** DT8 3EQ.

Refreshments Beaminster has a wealth of good places to eat, including tea rooms and excellent pubs.

The Walk

1 Return to the car park entrance. Bear right down the lane then turn left to a fork in the road. Take the right-hand road (**Fleet Street**) which leads to the square.

2 Cross the road and keep ahead with shops close on your right. On your left, in the centre of the square, is a covered market cross known as 'Julia' erected in 1906 by Vincent Robinson of nearby **Parnham House** in memory of his sister. Continue ahead and walk down **Church Street.**

3 Turn right. The church gates are on your left. The splendid church is full of interest. Don't miss the beautiful 19th-century rood screen. Figured on the west face of the 15th-century tower are delicately carved scenes from the Bible. Follow the lane ahead, passing **Church Cottage** on your right. Pass a road on your right and keep straight on along the grassed-over track ahead between high hedges and walls. You are following the route of the **Wessex Ridgeway Trail**. As it crosses Dorset, the route for walkers and horse riders is signed with wooden arrows with upward-curving points. You will see them along our route.

4 Cross a lane and go through a gate. A narrow footpath leads ahead over the grass with a stream down the bank on your left. Go through a gate to **Half Acre Lane**.

5 Turn left to leave the route of the **Ridgeway** and walk up the lane.

DORSET *Year Round Walks*

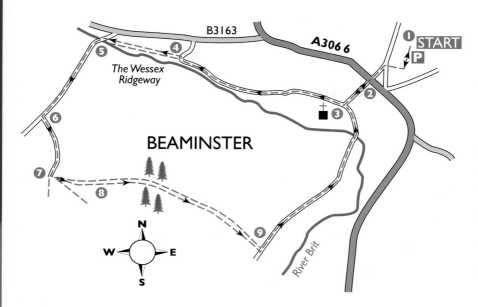

❻ As you near the top of the rise you come to a signpost on the left. Turn left following the yellow arrow footpath sign. Follow the narrow path ahead between hedges. You are high on the hill now, with wide-spreading views. Over the fields and low hills on your right rises the cone-shaped **Gerrard's Hill** crowned with trees.

❼ When the path meets a hedge, cross the stile and turn sharp left to walk up the field to enter one of Dorset's loveliest woods.

❽ Follow the path as it weaves its way through the trees keeping the edge of the wood about 40 yards away on the left. The path descends steeply and continues down steps to a small wooden gate. Go through the gate to leave the wood and walk down the field ahead. Half-hidden in trees, **Beaminster** lies in the valley on your left.

❾ The path descends to a track. Turn left through a gate and follow the path along the valley with a fence on the right. Go through a gate and follow the clear track which leads downhill before becoming a lane which bears left to the top of **St. Mary Well Street**. Turn right up **Church Street** to retrace your steps to the car park. As this is a short walk, I hope you will find time to explore this fascinating old-world town.

Our path leaving Beaminster.

What to look out for –

The Wessex Ridgeway

The trail is a magnificent ridge-top route running for 136 miles from Marlborough in Wiltshire over the hills and valleys of the Dorset downs to the coast at Lyme Regis. It is a wonderful walk with splendid views passing through many attractive villages. In Dorset, apart from the upward-curving arrows you will see on this walk, the route for walkers and horse riders is marked by circular discs with green lettering. In the centre of the disc there is usually a wyvern, a winged dragon with a snake's tail, a symbol dating back to King Alfred's Wessex. The trail follows the route of an ancient highway that was once an important trading route crossing the country from Devon to the Norfolk coast.

Canada geese arrive to spend the winter on the marsh.

12 Christchurch and Stanpit Marsh Nature Reserve

4.5 miles / 7.2 km

This superb walk starts in Christchurch, a historic town established by Saxon settlers before AD900. They chose an ideal site, at the head of a beautiful, almost land-locked harbour, protected to the west by the natural rampart of Hengistbury Head. Picturesque narrow streets cluster around the ruins of a castle built by the Normans. Dominating the town and the harbour is Christchurch's magnificent Priory Church. From the car park close to the Priory Church, this walk leads through the oldest part of the town to Stanpit Marsh Nature Reserve, a surprisingly remote wildlife area of almost 130 acres on the northern shores of the harbour. The route follows footpaths around the reserve. Salt and freshwater marshes, lagoons, sandy banks, gravel beds and large stands of reeds provide the right conditions for a wide variety of birdlife and autumn is a good time to see migrant species. The return route includes a lovely riverside walk.

The Facts

Terrain Easy flat walking. Could be wet in places, so wear strong shoes.

Map OS Explorer OL22 New Forest.

Starting point Christchurch Priory car park (GR SZ 160925).

How to get there Drive into the centre of Christchurch, and follow the signs for Christchurch Quay. Turn right in front of the pedestrian precinct before Christchurch Priory, then after a few yards, turn left to drive into the Priory car park. **Sat Nav:** BH23 1BU.

Refreshments Christchurch has excellent cafés and restaurants. You can also take a picnic to enjoy while admiring the view from one of the seats in Stanpit Marsh Nature Reserve.

autumn

The Walk

1 With the **priory** on your right, leave the car park by the entrance gates. The old house on the right was the porter's lodge, one of the few monastic buildings not destroyed during the Dissolution of the Monasteries in 1539. The Priory Church dates from 1094 and was part of the monastic buildings completed after 1150 for the Augustinian or Black Canons. Fortunately this beautiful church survived the Dissolution, claimed by the townspeople as their parish church.

2 Just past the porter's lodge, turn right to follow the good path diagonally across the churchyard in front of the priory. Go through the gates into Church Street. Continue straight ahead to the corner of **Castle Street**.

3 Turn right along **Castle Street**. On the right you pass a half-timbered building inscribed 'twelfth century'. Now housing a perfumery, this was originally the Old Court House where the mayor and town dignitaries took their oath of office. Standing high beyond the perfumery you will see the ruins of the Norman Castle – built to last with walls ten feet thick! Cross two bridges over branches of the **Avon**.

4 Immediately after the second bridge, turn right into **Bridge Street Car Park**. Follow the footpath signed for '**Civic Offices and Leisure Centre**'. The path winds round the offices to the leisure centre car park. Keep ahead along the right-hand edge of the car park with trees on your right and follow the sign '**Stanpit via Priory View footpath**'. In front of the boatyard bear a little left

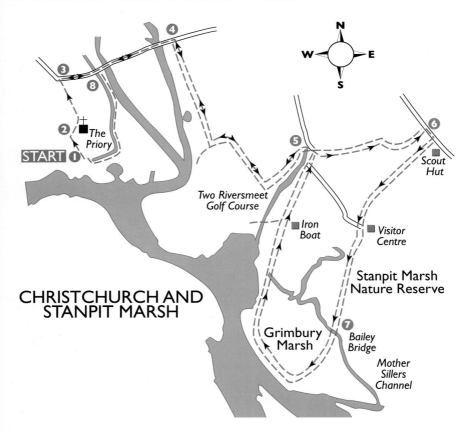

CHRISTCHURCH AND
STANPIT MARSH

Two Riversmeet
Golf Course

Iron
Boat

Visitor
Centre

Stanpit Marsh
Nature Reserve

Grimbury
Marsh

Bailey
Bridge

Mother
Sillers
Channel

Scout
Hut

The
Priory

START ❶

autumn

to continue along a narrow footpath with a hedge on the left. The path leads through a gate on your left, climbs some steps, then turns right around the edge of **Two Riversmeet Golf Course** following the fence on the left.

❺ Go through a gate to meet a narrow tarmac lane. Bearing very slightly right, follow the lane ahead past the blue cycle sign to **Stanpit Marsh car park**.

❻ Turn immediately right along the edge of the car park, pass the scout hut close on your right then turn right again round the scout hut. Follow an inviting path between thick hedgerows leading through gates into the nature reserve. This sheltered path provides homes for all our familiar garden birds and in summer and early autumn the ground is colourful with wild flowers. Beside the path you will see tall stands of teasels. Follow the path as it leaves the hedged way. A wide expanse of saltmarsh stretches before you, criss-crossed by channels alive with birds. Herons poise like statues beside the water and golden and grey

Boats on the Avon.

plovers peck at the mud with their short beaks. There are splendid river and harbour views and looking west the marshes extend so far it seems you could walk dry-shod to **Hengistbury Head**! The information centre beside the path is well worth a visit for leaflets and a map of the reserve.

7 The path leads across one of the few remaining Bailey bridges over **Mother Sillers Channel** down to the harbour shore. This prototype bridge was designed and built in Christchurch and was a vital innovation during the Second World War. The channel is named after a notorious 18th-century smuggling family who, like many others, made profitable use of these marshes. Follow the path as it curves right round **Grimbury Marsh** and heads north over small footbridges to a wreck known as 'the Iron Boat' which, during the Second World War, served as a United States Liberty ship. The path leads past a footpath on the left through a wooded area. Go through a gate and bear left to meet your outbound route at Point 5. Turn left to retrace your steps round the golf course, over the leisure centre car park and round the civic offices to **Bridge Street Car Park**. Turn left still retracing your steps crossing the two bridges over the **Avon**.

DORSET *Year Round Walks*

autumn

8 Just after the second bridge turn left to follow **Convent Walk**, a delightful path running between the **Avon** on your right and the **Mill stream**. Beside the Mill stream there is a rare example of 12th-century domestic architecture, the Constable's House, added to the castle for the resident warden. Although roofless, the walls are almost intact. Soon you come to a small medieval bridge on your right and close by you will see another of Christchurch's historic buildings, **Place Mill**. Though part of the monastic buildings, the mill was too useful to be destroyed. Now restored, the Mill is open for visitors. Cross the bridge and take the path ahead signed for the **Tricycle Museum** to return to the priory car park.

What to look out for –

The 'Miraculous Beam'

When the Saxons established their new town between the Avon and the Stour they called it 'Tweoxneam' later Twynham – 'the place between the waters'. A legend explains why this eminently suitable name was changed to Christchurch. Evidently the Saxons wished to build their new church

on St. Catherine's Hill, a mile north of the town. Materials were assembled there but each night they were mysteriously removed to the present site of the priory. Eventually the workmen accepted the new site and began building. Unfortunately one of the roof beams was too short and the disheartened workmen went home for the night. In the morning the beam was found to be the right length and fitted perfectly. The astonished builders recollected that there had been an extra workman among their number who never collected his pay. They believed this must have been the divine carpenter, Christ, so the town was renamed Christchurch. Look for the 'miraculous beam' over the arch at the south side of the Lady Chapel inside the priory established by the Normans on the site of the Saxon church.

View from Bladeley Hill.

13 Buckland Newton

3.5 miles / 5.6 km

Buckland Newton is a small village in a beautiful setting on the southern fringes of the Blackmore Vale. The scattered houses and cottages are overlooked by gently rounded hills. From the church the route leads up Bladeley Hill to take a ridge path with breathtaking views over the Blackmore Vale. It seems as if the whole of the Vale lies at your feet! To return to the village the route follows Barnes's Lane, a track with more lovely views. The track is named after Dorset's famous poet, William Barnes, whose ancestor Thomas once lived in the village. A meadow path leads downhill to cross the Lydden stream and return to the church.

Terrain One short steep climb, then easy walking.

Map OS Explorer 117 Cerne Abbas & Bere Regis.

Starting point The Church of the Holy Rood, Buckland Newton (GR ST 687053).

How to get there Buckland Newton is just west of the B3143, midway between Dorchester and Sherborne. Turn for Buckland Newton off the B3143, and drive to the T-junction, passing the turning for Cranes Meadow on the left. At the T-junction, turn left towards the church, where there is room to park. **Sat Nav:** DT2 7BX.

Refreshments The Gaggle of Geese pub in Buckland Newton ☎ 01300 345249. Reopened April 2018 following refurbishment.

The Walk

1 With the church on your left, walk down the road passing the manor on your right. The road runs downhill and curves left past a grassy mound shadowed by a large tree. A plaque states that this was the site of the village pound where stray animals were confined. At the foot of the hill the road crosses the Lydden stream and leads to a Y-junction.

2 Turn right up the lane marked with a no-through-road sign. The lane rises gradually to pass **Knap Farm House** on the left. A few yards past the farmhouse you meet two bridleways.

3 Take the right-hand bridleway. (There is a signpost but it is buried in the hedge and illegible.) Follow the track as it climbs steadily up **Bladeley Hill**. As you gain height you are rewarded by beautiful views over the **Blackmore Vale** and the western downs. **Buckland Newton** lies cradled in the valley. Cross a farm track and keep ahead along the hedged path until you come to a track on the left with a large barn on the corner.

4 Turn left to pass the barn on your right. (There is no sign.) This ridge track runs high across **Bladeley Hill** to meet **Barnes's Lane**.

5 Turn left to follow this attractive way bordered with hedges and trees. Continue downhill past a gate and sign on your left indicating a bridleway. (This leads to **Ford Down Lane** but the gate opens to a meadow with no visible

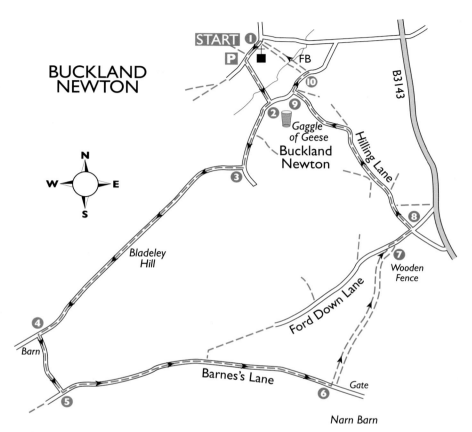

BUCKLAND
NEWTON

path.) Keep following **Barnes's Lane** until you see a small iron gate across the track on the left. A few yards before the gate a narrow track leads down to **Narn Barn** on the right.

6 At this point, turn left through a gate following the direction indicated by the yellow arrow footpath sign. Keep straight ahead over the grassy meadow with a hedge on your left towards the houses in the valley. The meadow slopes downhill. At the foot of the meadow go through a gate and keep ahead with the hedge still on your left. Cross a stile and continue ahead with a hedge on your right for a few yards then bear diagonally half-left towards a house to meet a wooden fence.

7 Navigate carefully at this point! Go through a gap in the fence and turn immediately left to cross a stile. Follow the narrow thickly hedged path to a road. Turn right and walk up to the crossroads.

autumn

8 Bear left, and follow **Hilling Lane** to a T-junction.

9 Turn right. As the road curves right look carefully for a small wooden gate on the left beside a larger wooden gate. The gates are just before a lay-by on the left.

10 Turn left through the small gate and walk down the field

View over Blackmore Vale from Bladeley Hill.

with hedges and trees on your left. Cross a footbridge over the **Lydden stream** and follow the thickly shaded path ahead to emerge in the churchyard. Pass the church on your right to return to your car.

What to look out for –

The Church of the Holy Rood

People have worshipped in this charming village church since the 13th century and the chancel dates from that time. The vaulted porch was built in the 15th century and over the door into the church you will see a 12th-century carving of Christ in Majesty.

Inside the church there is a much older piece of stone carving of a figure over the door. It was dug up in the vicarage garden and it could have belonged to a church built by the Saxons. A brass plate on the west wall commemorates in Latin the ancestor of William Barnes. When the church was reopened after restoration work in 1878, the famous poet attended the service.

A stone carving over the door dates from the Saxon 7th or 8th century.

Among the church's many delightful features is the little room with a fireplace above the porch, called a parvise. It is reached by a winding stair and was used in days past by monks and priests from Glastonbury when visiting the parish. If you look above the porch from outside the church you can see the window of the parvise.

Cottages in Trent.

14 ***Trent***

4 miles / 6.4 km

In north-west Dorset, close to the Somerset border, is a cluster of exceptionally attractive villages. One of the loveliest is Trent where this walk begins. The village lies in a valley just west of a range of limestone hills. Most of the houses and cottages were built of this local stone before the end of the 17th century and vary in colour from pale gold to deep russet. Little seems to have changed in Trent since the future Charles II, fleeing from the Parliament troops after his defeat at the Battle of Worcester, was hidden by Sir Francis Wyndham in the manor. From the church, the walk explores the village then follows part of the route taken by Charles along sunken, tree-shaded paths and lanes. You visit another attractive village, Nether Compton, before returning to Trent along an old cobbled way beside the Trent brook.

65

DORSET *Year Round Walks*

The Facts

autumn

Terrain Easy walking, but can be muddy after prolonged rain.

Map OS Explorer 129 Yeovil & Sherborne.

Starting point St Andrew's Church, Trent (GR ST 590185).

How to get there Trent is in North Dorset, close to the border with Somerset. The village lies two miles north of the A30, between Yeovil and Sherborne. From the A30, turn off following the sign for Over Compton. At the crossroads, go straight over, following the sign for Trent, and after about a mile, turn right for the village. Pass the church on the left, then turn immediately left; park on the left by the wall, at the approach to the churchyard. **Sat Nav:** DT9 4SL.

Refreshments The Rose and Crown, an old-world thatched pub in Trent, is very friendly, serving good food and drink ☎ 01935 850776. The Griffin's Head at Nether Compton is equally good ☎ 01935 812523.

The Walk

1 Go through the church gates and cross the churchyard to visit the church which is considered one of the finest in Dorset. Among much of interest, the church has preserved its magnificent 15th-century rood screen, pre-Reformation pews with intriguingly carved bench ends and a carved Dutch pulpit dating from around 1600. In the porch a notice requests that 'All persons are requested to take off pattens and clogs before entering'. If you walk up to the north-east corner of the churchyard and look over the wall on your right you will see part of the manor which sheltered Charles II. Retrace your steps, passing the chantry on your right. It was once the priest's house and is now a private dwelling.

2 Bear left from the church gates along the flagged footpath. You are now following the **Monarch's Way**, the route taken by Charles II. Just past Turner's Close – an attractive group of almshouses built in Tudor style clustered around a small courtyard – turn right following the sign for **Sherborne** and the village hall to walk through this picturesque village. Keep to the flagged footpath to pass the school on the right, the village stores and **Abel's Lane** on the left. About 100 yards further on the road curves left.

3 Keep straight ahead along the lane marked with a no-through-road sign. On the right you will see a small sign for **Down Farm**. Asphalted at first, the

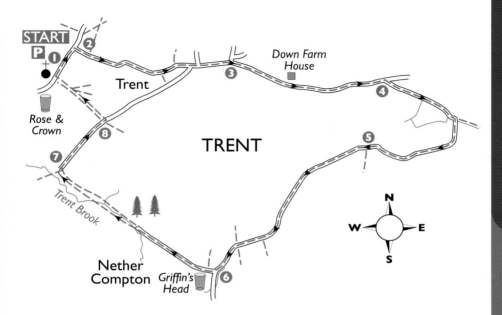

lane passes **Down Farm House** and becomes a grassy track running between high hedges festooned with honeysuckle in early autumn. Ahead rise green hillsides with small patches of woodland dotted in the hollows. Look for the **Monarch's Way** small circular signs on posts beside the track.

4 Keep to the track as it bears right past a small gate on the left leading to a path up the hill. Continue along the track. As you near the foot of the hill the track bears a little right and rises. Keep to the track as it turns right past a bridleway on the left. You leave the **Monarch's Way** at this point as it takes the bridleway. Our route traces the foot of the hills to pass a second bridleway on the left. Just past the bridleway the track meets a tarmac lane.

5 Follow the lane to **Nether Compton**, another attractive village built of glowing local stone.

6 At the junction turn right round the **Griffin's Head pub** and after about 50 yards, at **Crossfields**, take the footpath straight ahead following the sign for Trent. This delightful old cobbled way leads beside the **Trent Brook** to the mill, now a private house.

7 Turn right to follow a lane a little uphill to a signpost on the left. (Ignore

autumn

Autumnal colours on the Monarch's Way.

the sign for a bridleway on the right. You will see a very small footpath sign pointing left on the post.)

8 Turn left over a footbridge and go through an interesting iron gate. You pull it apart to open it! A footpath leads over the field ahead directly in line with **Trent Church**. As you cross the field you will enjoy a beautiful view. On the left is the long, low, thatched roof of the **Rose and Crown** and, to the right of the church, a glimpse of the **Manor**. Go through a gate to the road and turn right to return to the church and your car.

What to look out for –

The Monarch's Way

The way is a long-distance trail following, as far as possible, the route taken by Charles II as he attempted to escape to France after his heavy defeat at the Battle of Worcester in 1651. It runs from Worcester via Bristol and Yeovil to Brighton. Sir Francis Wyndham hid Charles in Trent Manor for 19 days. During that time Charles made two attempts to escape to France. He failed on his first attempt. A ship was waiting for him at Lyme Regis but the captain's wife prevented her husband from boarding! By the time Charles succeeded, sailing from Shoreham, he had seen a good deal of Dorset which he considered – surprisingly perhaps in his case– a very fine county. The sign for the trail, which you will see on this walk, shows the ship which took him to France (*Surprise*, a coastal brig which made a detour to land him in France), the crown with the Prince of Wales feathers and the oak tree in which he hid from Cromwell's troops at Boscobel. The route of the Monarch's Way was devised by Trevor Antill. He describes the waymarked route in detail in three volumes published by Meridian Books.

View over the downs.

15 Puddletown and Yellowham Wood

6 miles / 9.7 km

If you enjoy the novels of Thomas Hardy, this walk through some of the countryside which inspired him, to the cottage where he was born is a must. The route starts in Puddletown, a small village close to his home, which he called 'Weatherbury' in *Far From the Madding Crowd*. A great deal of the village was rebuilt in the 1860s when the rows of cob and thatch cottages were replaced by the stone houses we see today but some old thatched cottages remain clustered around the church. From the village you follow sheltered footpaths gradually climbing the downs and then descend through Yellowham Wood to Hardy's cottage. Hardy calls the wood 'Yalbury' and on the way you pass the keeper's cottage, the home of Keeper Day in his novel *Under the Greenwood Tree*. The route returns to the village through Puddletown Forest.

The Facts

Terrain Undulating paths, but generally firm underfoot.

Map OS Explorer 117 Cerne Abbas & Bere Regis.

Starting point Roadside parking beside St Mary's Church in Puddletown (GR SY 758944).

How to get there Puddletown village is about 4½ miles north-east of Dorchester. The village is well signed from the A35 and the A354. **Sat Nav:** DT2 8SN.

Refreshments The Blue Vinny pub near Puddletown, DT2 8TE ☎ 01305 848228. Hardy's Birthplace Visitor Centre, run by the National Trust, has a café with full facilities. The centre is about 200 yards down the road from Hardy's Cottage ☎ 01305 262366.

autumn

The Walk

1 With the north porch of the church on your left turn left along the signed footpath running between the church and the churchyard to the road. Turn right along the road passing the front of the Old School on your right as far as **Three Lanes Way**.

2 Cross the road and turn immediately left along a wide unsigned track leading ahead between high hedges. (Not the narrow signed path.) You pass the children's play area and cricket pitch on the left. Keep ahead through a gate past a path on the right to a tarmac lane. Follow the lane which bears left then right to cross the bridge over the dual carriageway.

3 Keep ahead following the sign for **Charminster**. The tarmac lane gives way to a grassy path between high hedges. The noise of traffic soon dies away as the path leads you gently uphill. Pass a bridleway on the left. As you reach the top of the down there are wide views over the rolling downs and woods beyond the **Piddle Valley** on the right. Continue past a track on the left leading to **Higher Barn** and **Troy Town Farm**. Perhaps Hardy named his irresistible Sergeant Troy in *Far from the Madding Crowd* after the farm. Follow the narrow path ahead which leads a little downhill and go through a small iron gate. At this point another bridleway runs diagonally across your path. Turn left and keep ahead for about 50 yards.

4 Navigate carefully here! Turn left along a narrow path arched over with

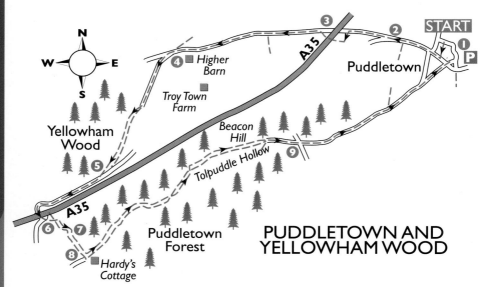

PUDDLETOWN AND YELLOWHAM WOOD

trees following the purple bridleway sign marked 'restricted byway'. Follow the path as it leads downhill through **Yellowham Wood** bordered by fine beech and oak trees. Here, Joseph Poorgrass, one of the most entertaining of Hardy's characters, out in the wood alone and possibly suffering from his 'multiplying eye' cried out, "Man-a-lost". Then, after an owl cried, "Whoo-whoo-whoo!" he answered, "Joseph Poorgrass of Weatherbury, sir!" As you near the bottom of the hill look carefully on the right through the trees. You will see a small thatched building which was the stable for the keeper's cottage. In front of the stable you will see the cottage, Keeper Day's home in *Under the Greenwood Tree*. One of the great trees close by could well be the greenwood tree which sheltered the guests who danced at Dick Dewy and Fancy Day's wedding.

5 When you reach the old road, turn right. The dual carriageway runs parallel along the embankment on your left. Bear left to cross the bridge over the dual carriageway. Turn left and just before the dual carriageway you will see a tarmac track on your right.

6 Turn right for a few yards up the track, then turn right through a gate into the woods. The path curves a little left then continues uphill.

7 About halfway up the hill the path becomes indistinct. Bear right and you will see the path more clearly leading ahead along a gully. Follow the path through the wood downhill to **Hardy's Cottage**.

8 Turn left following the sign for **Puddletown**. Keep ahead to cross the heath. The path now enters **Puddletown Forest**. The forest is dotted with pits and swallet holes where water disappears into the ground. Keep straight on, over all crosstracks. The path runs down beside **Beacon Hill** along **Tolpuddle Hollow**. This sunken way runs deep into the ground, its sides forming natural gardens of ferns and wildflowers. The path leaves the forest to meet a lane at **Beacon Corner**.

9 Follow the lane ahead towards **Puddletown**. At the fork take the right-hand lane and retrace your steps along the footpath with the church on your right to return to your car.

What to look out for –

Hardy's Cottage

You can combine a visit to the cottage with the route of this walk. (Access is via the visitor centre, a ten-minute walk from the cottage on the edge of Thorncombe Wood Nature Reserve.) The cottage, its homely cob walls faced with brick and rendered with cement, was built in 1800 by Thomas

Hardy's great grandfather for his son, also Thomas, who was a master mason. Hardy uses his cottage as the home of the Dewy family in *Under the Greenwood Tree*. Inside, the cottage has changed little since Hardy's time. The stone-flagged room with a low beam bisecting the ceiling, is just as described when it was the setting for the Dewy's Christmas party. The great inglenook fireplace where the young Hardy sat enthralled listening to country tales told by his grandmother dominates the room. Upstairs, in the small bedroom he shared with his brother Henry, Hardy wrote *Under the Greenwood Tree* and *Far from the Madding Crowd*. www.nationaltrust.org.uk/hardys-cottage

autumn

Following the Coast Path to Ringstead Bay.

16 Ringstead Bay
4.5 miles / 7.2 km

This is an exciting walk in one of the most remote and spectacular areas of Dorset's Jurassic coast. From the car park you follow a ridge of high downland with dramatic seaward views. The path then runs downhill past a tiny chapel, St. Catherine-by-the-Sea, perched on a grassy hillside, to meet the Coast Path and head west along the crest of Burning Cliff. The cliff marks the western end of a huge landslip of vertical boulders and crumbling vegetation covering 115 acres. It derives its name from the years between 1826 and 1830 when it burned almost continuously owing to the oxidisation of oil-bearing shale in its surface. You follow the path to Ringstead village and beach and see the mounds and embankments of a deserted medieval village before returning to the car park. This is a walk for any time of year but at quiet times in winter it is particularly enjoyable.

The Facts

Terrain Good undulating paths and tracks, with one short, steep climb.

Map OS OL15 Purbeck & South Dorset.

Starting point National Trust car park at South Down (GR SY 757825).

How to get there Turn south off the A352 Wool–Dorchester road at the Warmwell roundabout, and take the A353 to Weymouth. Soon after Poxwell, there is a sharp right-hand bend, followed by a tight left-hand turn onto a lane for Upton. Follow the lane through Upton; follow the sign for the National Trust car park, passing a turning for Ringstead and the beach café on the right (this is a toll road). Go straight on through a gateway, and park on the left of the track. **Sat Nav:** DT2 8NQ.

Refreshments The Smugglers Inn is a short drive away in the coastal hamlet of Osmington Mills. ☎ 01305 833125.

The Walk

1 The route of the first part of the walk from the National Trust car park is marked by orange arrows. Leaving a noticeboard on your right, follow the ridge heading south-east to a gate signed with an orange arrow and marked 'No Cars'. Go through the gate and continue downhill enjoying wonderful views over **Weymouth Bay**.

2 When you see a gate ahead bear right following the orange arrow sign down a track with a fence on your left to a wooden signpost.

3 Keep ahead downhill following the sign '**Coast Path and Ringstead**' also marked with an orange arrow to another signpost. Follow the sign for **Ringstead** to meet the **Coast Path**. (Our route is now indicated with the familiar acorn symbol.)

4 On the corner you bear right to follow the **Coast Path**, but before you do so you must see one of the highlights of this walk, the little chapel of **St. Catherine-by-the-Sea**. Turn left just past the corner to walk through part of the graveyard to see the chapel. Return to the **Coast Path** and continue downhill.

5 When the path divides keep ahead, following the **Coast Path** sign to follow

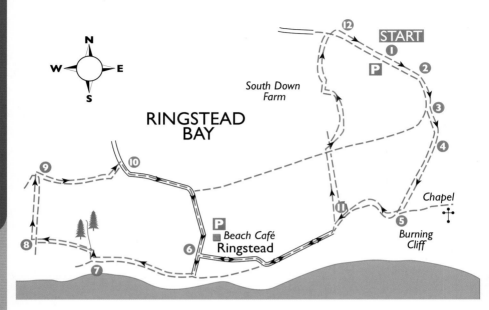

the crest of Burning Cliff. In his short story *The Distracted Preacher* about local smugglers during the Napoleonic War, Thomas Hardy suggests a different reason for the cliff's name. The heroine, knowing Customs officers are on watch, sets a gorse bush alight to 'warn off' an approaching ship full of contraband. Descend steps to cross two small footbridges following the sign for **Ringstead**. (Shortly after you pass a footpath on the right marked for **South Down** which is part of our return route.) Keep ahead to go through a small gate to a track which levels to pass a house on the left and approach **Ringstead** village. Keep ahead past a caravan site and houses on your left to a road.

6 The Beach Café is on the corner on your right. Turn left along the **Coast Path** through a gateway and bear right to follow the path running west above the beach past houses on the right. During the 18th century you might have spotted smugglers at work as the beach was a favoured landing place for contraband goods. They used a thatched cottage on the shore as their headquarters. The path bears a little left through a narrow wooded area then continues beside an open field with a fence on the right. If you look over the field you will be able to make out the low mounds of the site of Ringstead's medieval village. It is believed to have been destroyed by pirates.

7 Leave the **Coast Path** at this point and follow the footpath through woodland. Descend some steps and cross a stream. Climb the steps on the other side and follow the path through the woods to meet a track.

8 Turn right following the sign for **Upton** and keep ahead with the woods on your right to join a crosstrack.

9 Bear right for **Ringstead** through the woods. Go through a gate, bear left at the junction opposite **Glebe Cottage** and continue to a road.

10 Turn right and follow the road as it curves right and runs downhill to meet our outbound route at Point 6 opposite the **Beach Café**. Turn left to retrace your steps along the **Coast Path**.

11 After about a quarter of a mile, turn left to cross a stile signed '**N.T. South Down**' and marked with an orange arrow. Walk up the field ahead and go through a gateway. Continue along the track ahead beside fields with a hedge on your left. The track curves a little left then keeps on uphill before dipping down towards **South Down Farm**. Go through a gateway and pass the farm on your left. Follow the lane from the farm as it winds steeply uphill to the ridge path we followed at the start of the walk.

12 Turn right along the ridge to return to the National Trust car park and your car.

winter

What to look out for –

St. Catherine-by-the-Sea

This tiny wooden church has stood in a spectacular setting on the slopes of White Nothe cliff since 1926. It has been recently restored and is beautifully maintained. Although the church can only be reached by footpath it holds regular weekly services. Above the altar are three small engraved glass windows. If you have visited the church at Moreton and seen the windows engraved by Laurence Whistler you may recognise a family likeness as they are the work of his son, Simon. The hillside churchyard slopes down towards the sea. At the foot of the cliffs waves cream along the edges of inaccessible beaches and there are magnificent views over White Nothe and Weymouth Bay. Every year an outdoor service is held here in this lovely setting.

Looking west from the ramparts.

17 Eggardon Hill

2.5 miles / 4 km

Eggardon Hill is one of the most spectacular hillforts in Dorset. Situated on the western rim of the county's chalk uplands, the hill commands panoramic views over the Marshwood Vale and Lyme Bay as far as Dartmoor and Start Point in Devon. As you stand high on the fort's impressive ramparts all West Dorset is spread at your feet! A Roman road leads you to the start of this walk near the top of Eggardon. You take a footpath to the southern and western ramparts where you can wander at will and enjoy the stunning views before following a path over the hillfort. The whole of the centre of the fort is dotted with hut circles and traces of the large Iron Age settlement that once flourished here, dating back to around 300 BC. 'As old as Eggardon' is a local saying! This is a wonderful walk at any time of the year but, to experience the true atmosphere of this ancient hillfort, walk the ramparts in Winter. But be warned! Eggardon has many ghosts, including a phantom lady hitchhiker. As you drive away a glance into your rear view mirror might reveal her sitting in the back of your car!

The Facts

Terrain Undulating along the ramparts; otherwise flat.

Map OS Explorer 117 Cerne Abbas & Bere Regis.

Starting point Lay-by at the top of Eggardon Hill (GR SY 546942).

How to get there From Dorchester, take the A35 towards Bridport. After about three miles, the road drops downhill towards Winterbourne Abbas. Just before it does so, make a sharp right turn onto King's Road at Sunnyside Farm; then turn left, following the sign for Compton Valence, and follow Roman Road to the crossroads at the top of Eggardon Hill. Turn left, following the sign for Askerswell; after 200 yards, park in the lay-by on the left of the road. **Sat Nav:** DT2 9EP.

Refreshments The Spyway Inn near Askerswell ☎ 01308 485250.

The Walk

1 From the parking area walk back up the road for a few yards to the footpath sign on the left of the road. Go through a gate and follow the footpath which runs along the crest of the hill towards the ramparts of the hillfort.

2 At this point you come to a meeting of the ways. Do not go through the farm gate on your left marked with a white arrow bridleway sign. This path traces the foot of the ramparts then runs steeply downhill. Instead cross the small stile beside the gate and climb the ramparts to enjoy the marvellous views. The southern and western slopes of Eggardon are owned and managed by the National Trust and open for all to roam. It is a good idea to take a map with you to help identify some of the beautiful scenery. Looking west, the sea glints beyond the summits of **Thorncombe Beacon** and **Golden Cap** and overlooking the **Marshwood Vale** you will see Dorset's highest hill, **Pilsdon Pen**, and the wooded slopes of **Lewesdon Hill**. It is not surprising that the county's most notorious smuggler, Isaac Gulliver, who at one time owned Eggardon, planted fir trees on the top to act as a beacon for his ships loaded with contraband. Follow the ramparts until they descend a little to meet a fence on your right.

3 Retrace your steps to return along the ramparts and climb the small stile at **Point 2**.

4 Cross the large stile on your left marked with a yellow arrow footpath sign and walk up one of the entrances to the hillfort. The fence across the hilltop on

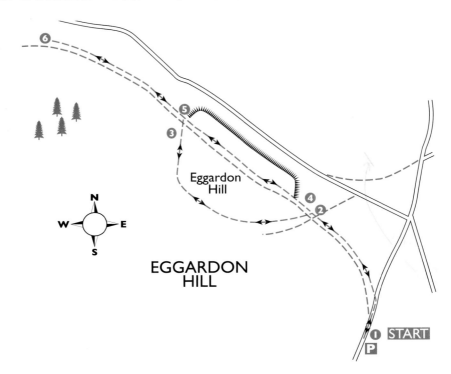

your left is an ancient boundary. The path curves a few yards left then continues across the centre of the fort. Today it is a peaceful scene, skylarks sing overhead and the short grass is starred with wild flowers in summer, but once the hill must have been alive with the noise of people and animals!

5 The path crosses the north-western ramparts and continues along the top of the steep hillside. Along the foot of the hillside you will see a green valley dotted with woods. There is a good chance of seeing deer. As the hilltop narrows the path ends in dense scrub. Look down into the valley beyond the fence on your left to see the **Bell Stone**, a small isolated rock in a beautiful setting. The stone has had a mysterious past. The old name for the stone was 'Bel Stone' taken from the Celtic god Belinos known as the 'Bright One' whose powers fertilised the land in spring, but an alternative version claims Belinos was a god of the Underworld which accounts for Eggardon's many ghosts!

6 Retrace your steps along the hilltop to continue along the path across the fort over the stile at **Point 2** to return to your car.

Looking west from the ramparts.

What to look out for –

Isaac Gulliver – 'the gentle Smuggler'

The southern slopes of Eggardon Hill fall away steeply to North Eggardon Farm. During the 18th century it was the home of Isaac Gulliver who also

owned Eggardon Hill. He was known as 'the gentle smuggler' because he claimed that no revenue man was ever killed during encounters with his men. The smuggling of highly taxable goods such as spirits and tea from the continent was a well organised business along the Dorset coast during the 18th and early 19th centuries and Isaac Gulliver is still remembered today! Quick-witted, utterly fearless, and a born organiser, he led a small army of about 50 men. They dressed in a special livery and were known as 'Whitewigs' from their powdered hair. Hair powder, fashionable at the time, was very heavily taxed! His last run was in 1800 after which he spent a long and dignified retirement as a respected citizen in Wimborne Minster. The fir trees he planted on Eggardon were quickly felled by the Customs men.

The 17th-century manor at Hinton St Mary.

18 Hinton St Mary

4 miles / 6.4 km

Hinton St Mary must be many people's idea of a traditional English village with a fine church, a 17th-century manor house and an excellent inn! The village stands on a low limestone ridge with wide views west over the Blackmore Vale. Below the village the River Stour winds its way between grassy hills and small thickly-hedged fields. The history of the village dates back to the third century when a Roman villa was discovered there in 1963. From the village, footpaths lead you downhill to the banks of the Stour. The route continues beside the river for about a mile to Cutt Mill providing a chance to see some of the river's rich wildlife including herons and kingfishers and, if you are very lucky, otters. Sadly, the mill is now a ruin but the millpond fed by the river tumbling noisily over the weirs is still impressive. Woodland and field paths lead back to Hinton St Mary.

winter

The Facts

Terrain Mainly flat, easy walking, but be prepared for mud after heavy rain.

Map OS Explorer 129 Yeovil & Sherborne.

Starting point St Peter's Church, Hinton St Mary (GR ST 787162).

How to get there Hinton St Mary is beside the B3092, a mile north of Sturminster Newton. Approaching from Sturminster, drive into the village and take the first minor road on the right, which leads up to the White Horse Inn. Approaching from the north, drive into the village and take the second minor road on the left. Turn for the church opposite the White Horse, and park by the church. **Sat Nav:** DT10 1NA.

Refreshments The White Horse Inn, Hinton St Mary ☎ 01258 472723.

The Walk

❶ The church has a 15th-century tower and inside you will find a monument to Thomas Freke who built part of the nearby 17th-century manor house on the site of a medieval monastic building. Leave the south porch of the church on your left and walk over to the corner of the graveyard. From here you have a good view of the manor overlooking classically-inspired gardens. Leave the church on your right and walk up to the minor road to face the **White Horse Inn**.

❷ Turn left along the raised pavement, passing the **Millennium Garden** on your right. Cross the main road, the B3092, and walk down the lane ahead.

❸ As the lane curves right, turn left along a track signed for **Sturminster Newton** passing private woodland on your left. The track may be obscured as it enters farmland but bear a little left to walk down the side of the field with the woods of **Twinwood Coppice** on your left.

❹ After about half a mile, when the woodland curves right, look carefully for a narrow path marked with a yellow arrow footpath sign entering the woods on your left. Turn right along the path through the wood and cross a small bridge to go through a gate. Keep straight on over the grassy hillside ahead.

❺ After about 150 yards, look down the hillside on your right for a small wooden bridge. Turn right downhill, cross the bridge, and bear right to join the

winter

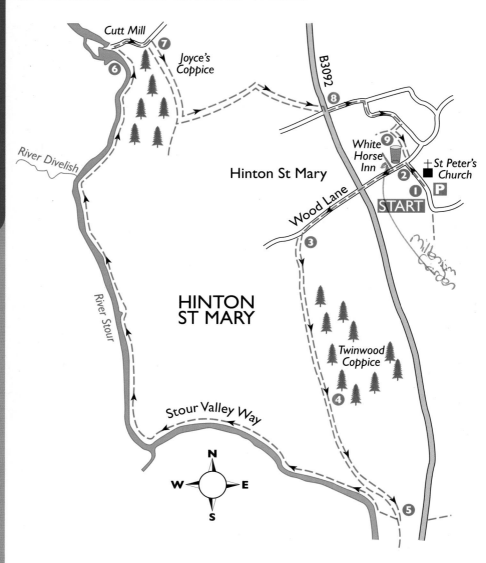

Cutt Mill

7

Joyce's
Coppice

6

B3092

8

White
Horse
Inn

9

St Peter's
Church

2

River Divelish

Hinton St Mary

1

P

START

Wood Lane

3

Millennium garden

HINTON
ST MARY

River Stour

Twinwood
Coppice

4

Stour Valley Way

5

N

W · E

S

Stour Valley Way, following the riverside. The river, fringed with thick stands of rushes, flows through the fields on your left. Where the branches of trees overhang the river look for the quick colourful dash of a kingfisher. Keep to the riverside path over bridges and through gates. Just past the point where the **Divelish** stream joins the **Stour**, the river curves right. The riverside path leads towards the trees of **Joyce's Coppice** then bears a little left to continue close

The Sluice Gate at Cutt Mill.

to the river with the trees on the right. The path then runs uphill through the coppice past a house on the left to meet a lane at **Cutt Mill**.

6 Turn left down the lane to see **Cutt Mill** in its beautiful setting. Although the mill is now a ruin the millpond, fringed with bulrushes and irises, is still lovely. William Barnes, the Dorset poet, came here to play as a boy from his home, **Rushay Farm** which was nearby. Retrace your steps up the lane passing your earlier footpath on the right.

7 A little further on, turn right following the bridleway signed for **Wood Lane**. When the track curves left keep straight on to leave the wood and enter a field. Turn left and walk to the corner of the field where the path turns right with a hedge on the left. After about 50 yards, look carefully for a yellow arrow footpath sign marking a narrow path through the hedge on your left. Follow the path and cross a stile. Bear half-right to the corner of a field in front of a group of buildings and go through a farm gate to meet a track.

8 Turn left, cross the B3092 and continue up the lane ahead to a joining lane on the right. Turn right and follow the lane as it curves left, then right, past houses until you come to a tempting signed footpath on your right.

9 Turn right and follow the hedged footpath and at a division bear left to continue past the side of the **White Horse Inn** to the road. Cross the road and walk back to the church and your car.

What to look out for –

The Millennium Garden

The Millennium Garden is charming. It was featured by the BBC in their programme *Charlie's Garden Army* presented by Charlie Dimmock, who spent a good deal of time helping a team of village gardeners in its construction. Features include a sundial, a small maze and an engraved commemorative seat. The sundial is unusual and fun. It consists of a circle five metres in diameter around which slabs are laid for every hour of the day. Slabs in the centre mark the months of the year. If you stand on the appropriate month your shadow tells you the time! The garden path leads into a cider apple orchard. The trees, old Somerset and Dorset varieties,

The Maze in the Millennium Garden .

were donated by Tom Denny. The artist lived in the village at that time. As you leave the garden, a large board gives details of the Roman villa discovered at Hinton St Mary in 1963, including the splendid mosaic floor which is believed to include one of earliest known portraits of Christ.

Gussage All Saints.

19 Gussage All Saints

6 miles / 9.7 km

This exhilarating ramble in the southern uplands of Cranborne Chase is the perfect walk for a bright winter's day as there is so much of historic interest to enjoy. From Gussage All Saints, an attractive village hidden away on a fold of the downs, you follow wide tracks used in the past by drovers, to the top of Gussage Down to be rewarded by a wide view north over Wiltshire. Part of the route follows Ackling Dyke, built by the Romans in the first century AD. The road would have been a busy highway noisy with chariots and troops travelling between Old Sarum just north of Salisbury and Durnovaria, today's Dorchester. A ridge path leads you west past the mounds and ditches of a large Celtic village probably dating from around 300BC. Close by are two well-preserved Neolithic long barrows. These large communal tombs are reminders of an earlier people, the first farmers. Today, the downs have returned to nature. The woods are the haunt of roe deer and all the way larks soar and sing overhead. More drove roads lead back to Gussage All Saints.

DORSET *Year Round Walks*

Terrain Good grassy tracks, but the first part of the walk can be muddy after heavy rain. Some gentle climbing.

Map OS Explorer 118 Shaftesbury & Cranborne Chase.

Starting point In front of the churchyard wall beside Harley Lane in Gussage All Saints (GR ST 999108).

How to get there Gussage All Saints is about seven miles east of Blandford Forum. Turn for the village off the A354 Blandford Forum–Salisbury road. Drive through Gussage St Michael. Then bear left over the bridge into Gussage All Saints. Do not follow the road as it curves right through the village; instead, go straight ahead into Harley Lane, passing the War Memorial on your right. There is room to park beside the churchyard wall on your left. **Sat Nav:** BH21 5HD.

Refreshments The recently reopened Drovers Inn in Gussage All Saints ☎ 01258 840550. The inn is owned and run by the local community, who also own the former school (bought from the Council for £20).

The Walk

1 Park in **Harley Lane** beside the wall of the churchyard. Leaving the church on your left, walk up **Harley Lane**. Just past the church you will catch a glimpse of **Manor Farmhouse**. Until 1920 it was the venue for the courtroom with the drawing room used for discussing smallholders' rights. On your right you pass **College Farm**. The track rises gently between high banks and the asphalt gives way to grass and gravel. After about half a mile, the track levels to give splendid views south-west over the **Gussage Valley**, then runs uphill once more.

2 After a short descent, turn left down a narrow path leading downhill to meet a wide thickly hedged track – a real drovers' track bordered with plenty of grass for their animals to graze as they were driven to market. Turn left to follow the track uphill and keep to the track as it curves right to lead still uphill towards the trees of **Burtt's Harley**.

3 When you reach **Burtt's Harley**, follow the track as it turns left to wind its way beside the wood which is on your right.

4 As you near the edge of the wood the track leaves the trees and bears a little left through a gate to lead beside a meadow with a hedge on the left. Over the

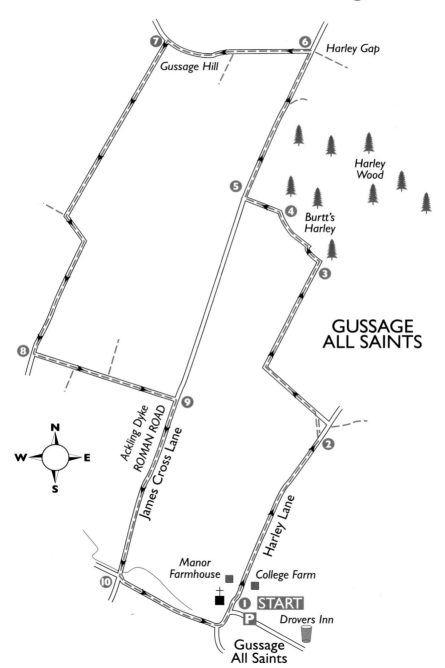

Harley Gap

Gussage Hill

Harley
Wood

Burtt's
Harley

winter

GUSSAGE
ALL SAINTS

Ackling Dyke
ROMAN ROAD

James Cross Lane

N
W   E
S

Harley Lane

Manor
Farmhouse

College Farm

START

Drovers Inn

Gussage
All Saints

winter

The stream flowing through Gussage All Saints.

meadow you will see a long line of embankments marking the route of the Roman road, **Ackling Dyke**.

5 Go through a gate and turn right to follow **Ackling Dyke**. Originally it would have been carefully planned to allow ten legionaries to walk abreast. Time has worn the road down but the high embankment on your left gives some idea of its former height. The road leads up **Gussage Down** to a junction of several tracks at **Harley Gap** marked by a wooden signpost.

6 Turn left to follow the fenced ridge path running west along the top of **Gussage Hill**. After about quarter of a mile, look over the meadowland on your right to see the site of the Celtic village. The surviving earthworks are very slight but it is not difficult to imagine the fields dotted with the circular huts of these Iron Age people. Dominating the skyline ahead you will see a large **Neolithic long barrow**.

7 Before you reach the long barrow the fence on your left turns left and our way leaves the ridge path to run south beside it. The ridge path continues heading west and if you pause for a moment to look along it you will see another long barrow which has been raised within the banks of the Dorset Cursus. The cursus originally enclosed 220 acres and the labour and tribal organisation involved in its construction must have been immense! Follow the grassy drove road beside the fence down **Gussage Hill** passing another prominent long barrow on your right. The track curves left then right as it continues downhill to meet a gravelled farm track.

8 Turn left up the gravelled track and when it curves left to cross a field keep straight on up the grassy track ahead. (You will see the roof of a building at the top of the slope.)

9 Rejoin **Ackling Dyke** and turn right to walk down to the lane to **Gussage All Saints**. As you join the lane you will see an information panel on the right.

10 Turn left to follow the lane back to the village, turning left at the signpost to cross the **Gussage stream** and return to your car.

winter

What to look out for –

Ackling Dyke

Ackling Dyke is one of the many Roman roads that survive today, often running beneath our modern highways. The Romans believed in building roads to last! Deep ditches were dug either side of the proposed route and the earth from the ditches was heaped in the centre. Large heavy stones were placed on top as a foundation. This was surfaced with a rammed layer of fine aggregate made from the best locally available material. For Ackling Dyke the Romans used flint beach pebbles brought from nearby Pentridge Hill. Some Roman roads in England have survived in almost their original state. Perhaps the most remarkable crosses Blackstone Edge on the high moors above Rochdale in Lancashire. Another well-preserved road crosses part of the North York Moors near Goathland.

Following the footpath beside the River Frome.

20 *Wareham*

4.3 miles / 6.8 km

Dorset has more than its share of small, friendly market towns and Wareham, where this walk starts, is one of the most charming. It is guarded to the north, east and west by its walls; high embankments raised in the ninth century to protect the inhabitants from Viking invaders. To the south the town is protected by the watermeadows of the Frome. North of the town the Piddle winds through wide expanses of reeds and marshes to meet the sea in Poole Harbour. This walk includes rambles in both river valleys. From Wareham you head east along a raised path following the meanders of the Frome to the mouth of the Wareham channel at Swineham Point. The path leads north before turning west to return to Wareham over the rough grassland of the Piddle Valley. These watery worlds are a paradise for birdlife. Curlews call over the marshes and kingfishers nest in holes in the soft clay of the river banks. Thick stands of rushes provide food for water voles and hiding places for otters. This walk is particularly rewarding in winter when there is every chance you may see rare winter visitors such as avocets.

Terrain Mainly flat, easy walking, but the riverside paths can be muddy and slippery after heavy rain. In that case, it may be a good idea to wear wellingtons with a good grip.

Map OS Explorer OL15 Purbeck & South Dorset.

Starting point Connegar Lane long-stay car park, Wareham (GR SY 925872).

How to get there Approaching from the north, turn for Wareham off the A351 along the B3075. Drive straight ahead into the town, and turn left into East Street. Shortly afterwards, turn right into Church Street, and take the second turning on the left, Church Lane. Turn left into Conniger Lane; the car park (spelt differently!) is on the left. **Sat Nav:** BH20 4NQ.

Refreshments Wareham has a good selection of pubs and tea rooms. You can enjoy excellent cream teas at one of the cafés on the quay while watching the boats go by.

The Walk

1 Turn left from **Connegar Car Park** and follow the sign for the **Two Rivers Walk** to follow **Conniger Lane** (it is spelt differently) heading east between the graveyards of **Lady St Mary Church**. On your right you will see the tower of this ancient minster church. In a small medieval chapel south of the nave the body of King Edward was laid for a year after he was martyred at Corfe by his stepmother in AD 978.

2 At the end of the lane the **Two Rivers Walk** is signed. Turn right following the sign for the **Two Rivers Walk** and **Swineham Point**. Follow the narrow footpath down to a large metal gate in front of a caravan site. Turn left along a narrow footpath with trees on your right. The path bears right with a board fence at first on the left to lead over a bridge and boardwalks, signed for the **Frome Valley Trail**. On either side dense stands of rushes border the path providing a home for reed and sedge warblers. A final boardwalk brings you to the raised path beside the **Frome**.

3 Bear left to walk beside the river which is on your right. Today, the river flows peacefully between its marshes and watermeadows providing a playground for pleasure boats but once the scene would have been very different. Until the end

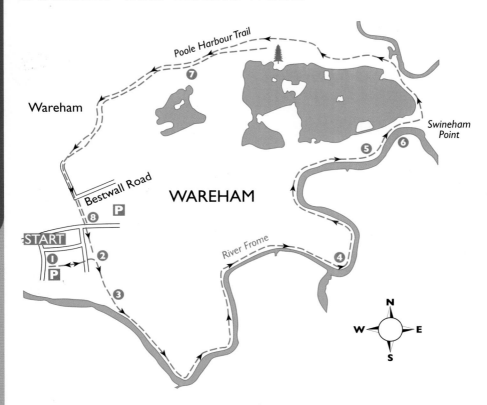

of the 13th century, when the gradual silting of the river made it impassable for large craft it was an important part of the trade route for the export of Purbeck ball clay. Originally the clay was brought by packhorse from the pits to the wharves at Wareham to be loaded onto barges and taken to Poole.

4 After about three quarters of a mile, look across the river to see the marina which marks the site of the wharves which once lined the waterside at Ridge. In 1830, the Furzebrook Railway was built connecting the wharves to the clay pits. This was soon superseded by road haulage.

5 As the river approaches **Swineham Point** it runs close to a large flooded gravel pit, a haven for birdlife and noisy in winter with the harsh cackling of Canada geese.

6 Beside a small jetty you come to a signpost. Turn right following the sign '**Swineham Point 197 yds**'. Keep to the path as it curves left round the point with a wide view eastwards over the mudflats towards **Poole Harbour**, a narrow blue line on the horizon. In winter this is a good place to look for marsh harriers. Follow the path round between hedges. Go through a gate to head west over the flood plain of the **Piddle** with trees and hedges on your left and open tussocky grassland on your right. The path bears a little right, still following the line of trees to a large iron gate on your left.

7 Turn left to go through the small gate beside the large gate and turn right to follow a track through woodland. This is a public footpath running through a private estate owned by the RSPB. Below the trees on the right the woods slope down to a valley where you may see roe deer. Go through a gate to continue along the woodland track to meet a lane. Turn right and follow the lane through more gates. Soon you will see the embankments of **East Walls** ahead. With the walls on your right, walk along the lane to a T-junction. Follow the sign for the **Frome Valley Trail** and the **Two Rivers Walk**, and cross **Bestwall Road**.

8 Climb the embankments ahead and walk along the top to enjoy the view. When you come to a dip, descend the embankments and continue along the lane. Turn right between the graveyards to return to **Connegar Car Park** and your car.

What to look out for –

St Martin's Church

St. Martin's Church on North Walls is not far from the route and is well worth a visit. St. Martin's dates from the 11th century AD and is the oldest and most complete Saxon church in Dorset. The north aisle houses Kennington's famous full-length marble effigy of Lawrence of Arabia in Arab dress. While Lawrence was at

nearby Bovington Army Camp he visited Wareham frequently enjoying a cup of coffee at his favourite table by the window in Anglebury Tea Rooms. (The owners will show you a plaque on the wall commemorating his visits.) Wareham Town Museum in East Street has an excellent display devoted to Lawrence and his final years in Dorset. The church is open from Easter to October. If the door is locked the key can be obtained from A.F. Joy, a menswear shop in North Street.

OTHER TITLES FROM COUNTRYSIDE BOOKS

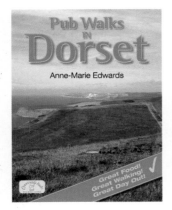
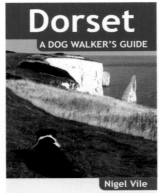
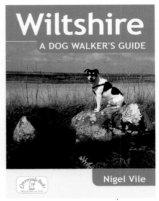

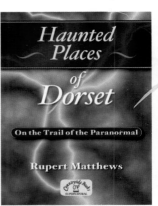
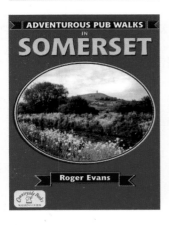
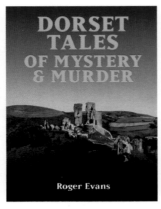
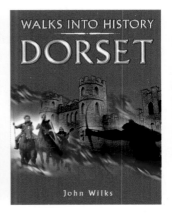